Scarcely Ever Out of My Thoughts

The Letters of Valda Trevlyn Grieve to C.M. Grieve (Hugh MacDiarmid)

With a Foreword by Deirdre Grieve
Edited and with an Introduction by Beth Junor

First published by Word Power Books, 2007.
This edition published 2008.
Word Power Books
43 West Nicolson Street,
Edinburgh, EH8 9DB
Tel 0131 662 9112
www.word-power.co.uk

Designed by Leela Sooben.
Printed and bound in Scotland.

ISBN: 978-0-9549185-7-6
British Library Cataloguing in Publication Data.
A catalogue record for this book is available from the British Library.

Illustrations
Cover image *Woman with Leaping Cat*, Robert Colquhoun (1914-1962) © Tate, London 2007.
The Bathing Pool, Bude, 1930s - original postcard from Bude Museum, courtesy the editor.
The Gilgal 1930s reproduced courtesy A.K. Bell Library, Perth.
The Gilgal today © Beth Junor reproduced courtesy the editor.
28 King Street today © Beth Junor reproduced courtesy the editor.
Newly discovered letter penned by C.M.Grieve (Appendix IV) reproduced courtesy Deirdre Grieve, with appreciation to Mr May of the Blanchminster Trust.
Letters reproduced courtesy Trustees of the National Library of Scotland.
Title page silhouette of Valda Grieve by Margaret Newell (1934). Despite our best efforts, we have been unable to trace the artist / her Estate. The publishers welcome information, for inclusion in future editions.

Acknowledgements

I would like to extend very grateful thanks and appreciation to Deirdre Grieve and her family for their permission to bring these letters into the public domain. As these letters deal with a living family, one can only imagine the many ways in which it cannot have been entirely easy to have them re-surface. Deirdre Grieve also made important corrections and added a considerable amount of information, employing great patience, all greatly appreciated.

Many thanks are due to John Manson, who, over and above his published work on MacDiarmid, always gave generously of his time to discuss matters, suggested solutions to particularly puzzling handwriting and read the final draft, supplying numerous additional details. For all of this I am extremely grateful.

I wish to express appreciative thanks to all who work in the National Library of Scotland, especially the Manuscripts Room staff. Robin Smith's interest and assistance were much appreciated. I am grateful to the Trustees of the National Library of Scotland for their kind permission to reproduce examples of the original letters.

The Authors' Foundation gave financial assistance which enabled me to buy time from my employer in which to make the initial transcriptions. This assistance was proffered without conditions or oppressive bureaucracy attached, that is, with respect for and trust in the work, and for this too I am very grateful.

I would like to thank the residents of King Street in Bude, Mr Cloke of Bude Museum and the staff at Bude and Launceston Libraries. Many thanks to Mr May, Clerk to the Trustees of The Blanchminster Trust, Bude, who took extra trouble to respond to my enquiries, thereby unearthing from the Trust's archives the two letters MacDiarmid had written on Valda's behalf. I am also very glad to have this opportunity to thank the helpful staff in the Local Studies department of the A.K. Bell Library in Perth.

Any errors are mine alone.

Contents

Foreword

If you were to meet the Valda whose observations and directions pepper these pages you would be struck by the assessing gaze, the already confrontational manner, the rich contralto voice and the assuredness of her spoken remarks in contrast to those she put on paper. All this after you had checked her hair colour. Orange.

Very soon, depending on her mood or her first impressions of you, you would be beguiled by her warmth or alarmed by her hostility, probably both.

Both these facets of her personality come through in this collection of letters even though they are one half of a running dialogue with the person for whom she had the most sustained and consistent of feelings. Her focus, her patience, her ambition, her huge capacity for affection were almost all tied up in Christopher.

It was very easy to warm to Christopher. His unwieldy intellect seemed to come at the expense of ease with simple things. The mechanics of daily life were automatic, and where not automatic ignored. There was a childlike element too in his bad behaviour, not always as spontaneous as it seemed, while in his directed, impersonal, political attacks he simply became another person.

Valda's capacity to absorb and balance all this, to turn their extremes into a domestic norm, was a rare talent. In her immense and ultimately successful effort to control their lives, to deliver her wayward husband to a comfortable, garlanded, almost mellow old age against the current of the deviant bohemian world in which they met and to which they continued, albeit as country members, to belong was her greatest achievement.

As Beth Junor points out it is more correct to say that they were poor than that they were deprived. The Valda whom I first met in 1957, the year before Michael (the 'James' prefix shed before his first teeth) and I were married, cooked on a range, carried pails of water and had an outside toilet furnished with shredded newspapers, before a group of St. Andrews University students built a kitchen and bathroom extension onto their cottage.

In their penny-counting days the Grieves had been lucky to have concerned and generous friends, not least the Tweedies on whose farm the but and ben Brownsbank Cottage was located and who let them have it rent free. After they became, by their standards, comfortably off, they in turn were generous and prodigiously hospitable.

Valda furnished the cottage with her own multi-coloured knitted and crocheted blanket-square curtains, cushions and bedspreads (visitors sat on the beds), with coloured glass fishing floats, bric-a-brac, paper flowers, drawings and paintings at a time when Scottish interiors were a monoculture of regency stripes and fawn uncut moquette. From September to May a fire blazed in the grate. Lunch guests might be asked to chop and fetch logs and to unfold the table which would soon be heaped with a sort of Cornish/French fusion of home-baked pies or pasties, little crackle glaze dishes of *crudités*, red wine in blue glasses, often preceded by a hearty meat-based soup whose secret ingredient was leftovers scraped from previous guests' plates.

Christopher, who drank whisky rather than wine with the meal, would suddenly rise and head, on autopilot, for the kitchen to do the washing-up, turning down offers of help. Duty done, he shared out the whisky. Valda opted for brandy, and instructed all but the most elderly and distinguished of guests to take her dog for a toilet stop walk, being careful to avoid fields of sheep. In summer they might spill outside. Allen Ginsberg was snapped sitting with them on the grassy verge of the lane outside the gate, after which Valda liked to tell new acquaintances "I've smoked cannabis with Allen Ginsberg, you know". In her eighties, she exchanged this for "Augustus John wanted to paint me" showing a flexible sense of market values.

The vulnerability that comes through in her letters is a particularly poignant and valuable memorial to her as she took care to show no trace of that in her dealings with friends and acquaintances.

For strangers she reserved her attack-as-best-form-of-defence behaviour. Well aware that with the passing of the decades her life's work no longer stood up in social circles, she was inclined to have a go at younger women with definable jobs on their *cvs*. If they stuck it out long enough for her to relax and see that they were not, or were no longer, about to patronise her, she could become a faithful friend. Women she suspected of having designs on her husband were another target, as were men she might politically disapprove of. At a party she threw the contents of her wine glass at Ian Hamilton Q.C., who as a student had stolen the Stone of Destiny, because, she told him, he had given it back. At another I stood beside her as she emptied someone else's pint beer glass over a young policeman, called by neighbours to sort out the noise, because… well, because it was a fun thing to do and he was a policeman.

Her life spanned a time when full-time domestic drudgery gradually made way for leisure, as did mine the final fling of that drudgery and the pioneering days of the working mother. With a job and a first child in the days before disposable nappies her imprecations to me to 'turn the collar' of Mike's shirts (to unpick and re-sew them) when they became worn and to soak his (pre-Kleenex) handkerchiefs before hand-washing them felt a little like being challenged to a duel with a broadsword.

The domesticity of these letters is surreal. Dirty socks and sheets speed from Shetland to Cornwall, pasties and saffron cake catch mail trains and boats across the Pentland Firth. All that threatens to be banal is tense with the never-expressed acknowledgement that this is not the way most people live.

Despite the evidence of the letters, the marriage of Christopher and Valda was not the simple marriage of chaos and harmony. Christopher was an orderly, essentially moderate man with an immoderate talent, who was also programmed to go off the rails. Valda was a free spirit who loved to stir things up, but whose destiny was to provide a peaceful environment for someone who would never be boring enough to make her reconsider.

Deirdre Grieve

Introduction

Hugh MacDiarmid was one of the greatest 'Western'[1] intellectuals of the twentieth century. A famous poet and speaker, political thinker, journalist, essayist, biographer, compulsive communicator in both letter writing and talking, always engaged in the public realm yet assiduously attending to detail (with less consistency) in his private realm, in a line of 'greats' from Scotland in international literary reputation he is a successor to Burns, Scott and R.L. Stevenson.

'Hugh MacDiarmid' was the pseudonym adopted in 1922 by Christopher Murray Grieve, born on 11th August 1892 to Elizabeth and James Grieve of Langholm, a small town in the Scottish borders a few miles east of the town whose name is now more commonly recognised, Lockerbie.

Christopher Grieve's marriage to Valda Trevlyn was his second. Having served in Greece and France in the First World War, in June 1918 he had first married Peggy Skinner. They had two children together: Christine, born in September 1924, and Walter, born in April 1928. In 1929 Peggy began seeing a man very much wealthier than Grieve, William McElroy. In 1931 Christopher and Peggy split up in the most bitter terms, with Christopher being denied access to his children, a situation which nearly completely broke him. The devastating effects of this were fully brought to light when the *New Selected Letters* of Hugh MacDiarmid were published in 2001. The events leading up to the divorce (which came through in legal terms in January 1932, in Edinburgh) are also fully documented in the *New Selected Letters*. Christopher was deprived of contact with his two children from this marriage for over twenty years, a situation unimaginable nowadays.

It was at this highly emotional time that MacDiarmid (known by this name since he had already begun to lead the Scottish Literary Renaissance, having published his collection *Sangschaw* in 1925, *Penny Wheep* in 1926, as well as

[1] The Egyptian intellectual Nawal El Saadawi has pointed out the limited, relative meaning of this term.

A Drunk Man Looks at the Thistle) first saw Valda Trevlyn at a literary evening in Hennekey's Bar in High Holborn, London – if she didn't take much notice of him then, he certainly did of her, lighting her cigarette every time she took one out and later arranging through a mutual friend to meet her again. Grieve would have felt at ease amongst his own crowd, whereas Valda thought the literary 'soirée' to which her friend had invited her along was 'a church meeting or something,' she later told Raymond Ross for his profile of her in the *Scotsman* newspaper, published six years after Christopher's death.[2]

His attitude towards woman is the basic point
A man must have thought out to know
Where he honestly stands.
Since praise is well, and compliment is well,
But affection – that is the last and final
And most precious reward any man can win.

from *Cornish Heroic Song for Valda Trevlyn (1939)*

Valda Trevlyn was born in Bude, Cornwall, on 1st July 1906. The 'Tre' prefix to her surname immediately identifies her as a Cornishwoman; she remained a Cornish Nationalist throughout her life. She was brought up in an all-women household, by her mother and Aunt Agnes (see Appendix II). Her father had died while she was still a baby.

After leaving school at 17, she worked locally until she was 19, then left home for Bristol. 'I had only been in a train or a café once before and I was frightened out of my life,' she told Ross. Here she worked as a shop assistant for 18 months, then left for London, where she had always wanted to be.

After their initial meeting, Grieve took Valda to Hennekey's again and they began to see each other regularly. The Plough, Bloomsbury, on the corner of Museum Street, was another of the pubs they went to - a stone's throw from The British Museum, whose British Library Reading Room (now preserved

[2] *Scotsman*, 1 September 1984. Valda's notes for this interview, corrections and outline for a planned autobiography are also in the National Library of Scotland. The biographical information here is from these sources.

as a museum – the new British Library opened in St Pancras in 1998) display lists 'Hugh MacDiarmid (Christopher Murray Grieve)' amongst the literary greats to have worked there. At The Plough again the crowd was very much Christopher's, including the editor of the *London New Age* A.R. Orage and his assistant Philippe Mairet[3], the French writer Denis Saurat whom Christopher would describe in 1939 as 'one of my oldest and best friends'[4] and Charlie Lahr of the Blue Moon Press and shop.

The couple moved out of London to the village of Thakeham in West Sussex[5] during Valda's pregnancy (which had been planned and which delighted Christopher). Their cottage had no running water and no furniture. Valda drew water from a 90-foot well and walked six miles for their groceries.

A neighbour advised Valda to see a doctor, which she eventually did a few weeks before delivery. The doctor advised hospital, but there being no beds in the charitable or voluntary hospitals of the time, she was taken into a private hospital run by a niece of Lord French, 'who took a couple of charity cases to eat up the left-overs' as Valda put it. James Michael Grieve was born on 28th July, 1932. Some weeks later, Valda was still in bed recuperating when Christopher appeared at the window during a violent thunderstorm, to let her know someone would arrive the next day with a message. This happened, the messenger explaining Christopher was on the run, evading both debt collectors

[3] Bashabi Fraser's *A Meeting of Two Minds: Geddes Tagore Letters* (Edinburgh: Word Power Books, 2005) includes interesting references to Mairet.

[4] *NSL*, p. 173.

[5] Christopher believed the cottage they stayed in was owned by Count Geoffrey Potocki de Montalk (*Lucky Poet*); the poet Count Potocki (b. 1903 in Auckland, New Zealand as Geoffrey Wladislas Vaile de Montalk, d.1997) had rented both the Thakeham cottage and a room in Hammersmith. His New Zealand friend Douglas Glass had been staying in the Thakeham cottage. Count Potocki and Glass were arrested for obscenity as a result of a poem the Count had tried to get typeset (he intended to print it himself for private circulation). '"Finally, a certain Scotch Nationalist, who wanted to lease a house I was renting in Thakeham – in addition to my room in London – in the event of my going to gaol, and was consequently willing to impress me with his wealth, bailed Mr Glass although he didn't know him from a soapy bar." The Scot was poet Hugh MacDiarmid.' – Stephanie de Montalk, in *Unquiet World The Life of Count Geoffrey Potocki de Montalk*, p. 137. The Count was imprisoned for 6 months. Stephanie de Montalk's chapters on the Count's ancestors – who included a mistress of Chopin - and on his arrest, trial and imprisonment, make fascinating reading. The Count had put it about London that he was an heir to the Polish throne; it seems he may have had a claim just as legitimate as many another aristocrat of Polish origin. Count Potocki's interest in genealogy is further reflected in his book *The Blood Royal of Ireland, Scotland, Wales, England & Other Countries* (Draguigan: The Mélissa Press, 1966), published 'as a smack in the Eye to the conceited, arrogant, and on the whole thoroughly mediocre present-day English Uppish classes.' – *Unquiet World*, ibid, pp. 30-31. The Count's perception of MacDiarmid's 'wealth' at the time may cast some doubt in readers' minds about the veracity of a few of his other beliefs.

and the police searching out a Breton nationalist he had been harbouring. Valda was discharged two days later and was taken to London, from where she and baby James Michael made a gruelling 17-hour journey to Scotland on the overnight bus. There had not been time, it seems, to register James Michael's birth, something which Valda attended to returning from a subsequent visit to her family in Bude, in July 1936.

The family were taken in by friends Robin and Mrs Black for two or three weeks, then stayed for a few months at Fruit Farm Cottage at Longniddry (1932-3). In one of her letters expressing her love for Christopher, Valda refers to an occurrence in Longniddry as the only time she had ever felt bitter towards him. They moved to Edinburgh for a short while, then when James Michael was around nine months old, Valda took their son back down to Cornwall to stay with her mother and aunts for a time; it is from this separation that her first letters to Christopher originate.

The Spring 2002 issue of the National Library of Scotland's magazine, *Folio*, carried an article by Alan Riach, 'Crying Out to be Written', outlining his involvement with the Hugh MacDiarmid archive and bemoaning the lack of any 'comprehensive social literary history of [*MacDiarmid's*] period.' This, he said, is a history crying out to be written: 'The history of the relationships of these writers and others – the composers and artists of the period ... . The archives of the Library are full of material demanding to be sifted and creatively interpreted ... the idiosyncrasies of his friendships and acquaintances, his intimate personal response to contemporary political events: knowledge of these helps humanise MacDiarmid and might subvert the process by which a poet becomes a caricature and a caricature becomes an icon. ...a more humanised comprehension of identity would help ... the letters of Valda, his second wife, are a wonderful, daunting repository, displaying her vulnerability and her protective devotion to her husband and son as well as her independence...' It was this article that prompted me to read Valda's letters. Initial searches of the National Library's catalogues yielded no entries devoted to Valda herself. All her entries were subsumed under MacDiarmid's repository (this is not the case today). When I read through the two main folders, I was so struck by the letters, I resolved to prepare them for wider public access.

At Brownsbank Cottage, the Grieves' last home, the Writer in Residence at the time - quite understandably - did not know of the letters' existence in the public archive. Brian Smith has a wonderful essay in *MacDiarmid in Shetland*, but even he admits, 'I have omitted some important things. There is not enough here about the way Valda worked hard, even when she was ill and dispirited, to keep the three of them alive.'

It is not difficult to bring to mind the historical context in which these letters were written when one comes across the naive and sympathetic treatment of Stalin. It is perhaps more difficult for post-war generations to imagine some of the other, more domestic, circumstances. When the pre-1948 letters were written, there was no National Health Service and no Social Security system, so that the illnesses and hospitalisations described would have incurred worrying medical bills seemingly impossible for the couple to meet, given their impecunious circumstances. In the post-war years when Valda threatens to go on Parish Relief, a last resort, Christopher would have felt how humiliating this would have been for her. Penicillin was not widely available until the Second World War period; likewise many treatment methods for infectious diseases, which we take for granted today, were non-existent and this, combined with worries over hospitalisation options when one had no money, meant rumours of a smallpox epidemic in Glasgow would have been of very serious concern indeed for Valda preparing to take James Michael there.

Women had less economic independence, therefore choices of partner were liable to be influenced by economic considerations. One such choice catalysed another branch of creative life at this time – one Christopher Grieve was close to, since it was Compton Mackenzie's invitation to be London editor for his weekly radio review *VOX* that had taken Grieve to London: William Walton was at this time writing his First Symphony, its composition fuelled by personal desertion and loss, not unlike Grieve's own experience, when the composer's beloved left him for a Hungarian doctor. The symphony's first performance was in London on 6 November 1935, when Grieve had just returned to Shetland from treatment for a nervous breakdown, which seemed to have been his own turning point regarding his first wife. Artists were not good choices, if one thought in terms of economic survival. Had Valda not been made of such strong stuff, had she been less curious intellectually, or already with young children, she would perhaps have determined – despite any emotional attachment – to give a wider berth to the impoverished poet and journalist she met in a London pub surrounded by friends who today would no doubt be branded 'extremists.'

The couple were desperately poor throughout their first decades together. Yet they survived somehow on very little materially and you will read how Valda particularly was anxious to protect their son from deprivations. They succeeded in this, so it is more correct to say that they were poor, rather than deprived. In fact, their son remembered the Shetland years as the happiest of his childhood.[6]

The postal system was much more impressive than today. There were two deliveries daily, and a letter posted in Bude, Cornwall in the morning could reach Shetland in less time and more reliably than it now often takes a first class letter to reach Edinburgh from London.

The references to money up until 1971 are pre-decimalisation and appear in UK Pounds, Shillings and Pence. In 1933, a stamp cost a penny ha'penny (1 ½ d), so Valda having to ask her family for money for a stamp (pp. 22, 26) would have been humiliating indeed.

Writers could make a meagre or even modest living being published by small publishers who not only believed in nurturing the ideas and craft of their writers but who were able to pay them something. Grieve, of course, also earned money from journalism. There were no Arts Council grants, i.e., there was less state control of creative life and hence a stronger collegiate attitude amongst writers. Intellectuals were even, on occasion, respected and listened to (if not always agreed with), that is, they had not yet been supplanted by experts and celebrities. It was still possible for ideas expressed in the public sphere to be in the form of well thought out and often lengthy argument, not merely in sound-bites. Furthermore it was assumed the audience or readers were intelligent, reflective adults, not Attention Deficit Hyperactivity Disorder sufferers with the language levels of primary school-age children.

Remember also, intellectuals were not an elite class from privileged backgrounds or academia – in keeping with Debray's study of French intellectuals, it was not the level of education that defined the intellectual but the 'project of influencing the public.'[7] Many intellectuals were non-consumers *sine qua non*. Sartre, of the same generation, who did have a more privileged upbringing than

---

[6] See Michael Grieve's Foreword to *MacDiarmid in Shetland* (Shetland Library); see also his introductory essay in *Hugh MacDiarmid Selected Poetry* (Fyfield Books/ Carcanet).

[7] Quoted in Frank Furedi's *Where Have All the Intellectuals Gone? Confronting 21st Century Philistinism*, p. 35.

MacDiarmid (whose father was a postman), nevertheless had a daily routine as follows: '... at 8.30 am he got up. From 9.30 am to 1.30 pm he would write. (Four hours in the morning and four hours in the evening, that was his only rule.) From 2.00-4.00 pm he would lunch in a café ... perhaps work there on some writing but certainly meet friends for conversation. Before 5.00 pm he would walk home and the second four-hour stretch of writing would be from 5.00 – 9.00 pm. At 9.00 pm he would typically walk to Simone de Beauvoir's flat and they would talk and listen to music. Sartre would be asleep by 12.30 am and, in the morning, would breakfast in a local café, between 8.30 and 9.30 am....Although he drank plenty of black coffee and smoked excessively, he drank very little alcohol. His social life took place in the afternoons. Three o'clock in the afternoon, he thought, was too late to finish anything and too late to start anything. The first volume of the *Critique of Dialectical Reason* was written at three times the normal speed because Sartre took twenty amphetamine tablets per day to finish it. Although he was physically strong, or perhaps partly because of it, Sartre took little care of his body. Sport bored him. He was happy to abuse his body to accelerate his written output. Sartre never owned a house or an apartment. For long stretches he would rent rooms in hotels. Indeed, his personal possessions were few: modest clothes, cigarettes, writing materials. When money came, say from Gallimard, he would carry all of it as a wad of banknotes in his wallet donating it copiously to friends or worthy causes. Michel Rybalka reports that on arriving to interview Sartre about *Critique of Dialectical Reason* they had to walk to a local bookshop to buy a copy.'[8] MacDiarmid's working habits were less routine, and he suffered physically and mentally for it – in Shetland it was commonplace for him to work all day and all night and in a sense the structure imposed by the years of industrial conscription in Glasgow physically saved him, although they were very limiting intellectually. In terms of the relationship of the intellectual to society, Sartre and MacDiarmid are a far cry from fulfilling today's publishers' concerns regarding the 'promotability' of an *author* (n.b. not his/her work). Indeed it is hard to believe either Sartre or MacDiarmid would be considered to have an image 'promotable' by today's celebrity standards.

When things improved financially for the Grieves, by 1967 Valda was able to write, 'We have everything we want, - domestically.' What a wonderful statement. 'We have everything we want' is an attitude of living that forms a solid foundation for a rich inner life. A society holding this anti-consumerism tenet in higher esteem, acknowledging the finiteness of the 'market,' would have a cultural life richer than any amount of Arts Council funding could achieve. When economic considerations dominate our cultural life, image is

---

[8] Stephen Priest, 'Sartre in the world', in *Jean-Paul Sartre: Basic Writings* (Routledge).

all, substance of little import. For this reason alone it is important to publish material such as these letters, to realise, in part, Alan Riach's vision of 'a more humanised comprehension of identity' of our cultural figures. Sometimes it is important to know more about what we have lost in order to regain it in contemporary forms.

Times have changed beyond compare similarly with publishing and bookselling, where take-overs of small publishers and booksellers by one combined company group are clearly against the public interest. Cut funding to libraries and allow the monopolisation of bookshops, and even reading becomes subjected to market forces.

Those who had to write did write and as a consequence there was no such thing as self-indulgence – it was always a matter of survival and, for MacDiarmid, compulsive communication. Certainly MacDiarmid did not indulge in the kind of arrogance some of today's writers display, for instance permitting an Agent to reply to correspondents that The Famous Novelist has just returned from a book tour, hence there will be no post forwarded whilst She is resting. This nurturing of self-indulgence, which serves the economic interests of the large bookstore chains, is simply a protection racket, destructive to a healthy balance of ego and any collegiate sense of responsibility. It is this collegiate sense of responsibility that supported MacDiarmid's writing, when the poet Helen Cruickshank encouraged Grieve to go to Shetland because it was a dry island. In doing so, Cruickshank performed a great service to Scottish cultural life and letters. MacDiarmid in turn was exceptionally generous in corresponding with others, throughout the years, regardless of his growing reputation.

Much more is known now about the neurological differences between male and female and concomitant discrepancies in the ability to assimilate and apply social information. Much more is understood about the learning and thinking styles of such intense, genius minds as MacDiarmid's, including the self-medication with alcohol or other drugs for purposes of productivity, socialisation or as the only perceived relief from the stresses of intense, prolonged mental activity (which are actually no greater than the stresses of other kinds of intense or prolonged labour). However, understanding brain organisation is one thing and living with a person quite another. I do not think anyone could have done a better job than Valda in teaching Christopher how to attend to practical considerations affecting others (including herself and their son), how to physically and mentally survive through a modicum of routine and attention to physical health, how to attend to practical matters relating to oneself that are also part of survival, in short, how to insist Christopher Grieve remain fully 'in this world' and connected to others (and hence have the capacity to express this in Hugh MacDiarmid's work). Christopher chose well when he saw Valda – I am sure he perceived from the start the qualities that were to help her survive their years of hardship, qualities that in turn were to sustain himself. Valda was the sustenance for Grieve's intellect and creativity.

Although these were stimulating and fascinating documents of social and literary history with which to work, at the same time, I was very moved by the letters. I was continually filled with admiration for both Valda and Christopher – Valda particularly for her unpretentiousness and strength of character, Christopher for his willingness to learn from Valda. Christopher Grieve responded to Valda's admonishments. (In this respect too MacDiarmid parts company from Sartre, who devised – and got away with – a whole intellectual rationale for shoddy treatment of women.) If his written responses were often in his most defensive mode, and accounting for the difference between the image one can paint of oneself on the page and real behaviours, they were always respectfully written responses which showed he had taken seriously what Valda had to say. Although the purpose here is to bring Valda's contribution and experience into view, there is, naturally, also much that will illuminate the character of Hugh MacDiarmid. It is the person – intellectual or not - who is unwilling or unable to develop in human terms in the way Christopher Grieve developed over the course of his relationship with Valda, that a character such as hers would undoubtedly have found intolerable.

Correspondence is a form of dialogue, but it is a structured dialogue, stripped of much of the spontaneity and of all the prosodic features of spoken conversation. Valda is aware of the ambiguity that results from stripping conversation of its prosodic markers. The prosodic features of spoken conversation (particularly pitch, pause, stress) convey a speaker's intent and at times she clarifies the feeling behind her message: 'This may seem light and bordering on sarcasm I assure it is not what I intend to convey to you,' for example (7th December 1933).

Valda saw herself as inarticulate and expressed frustration at times at being unable to express exactly what she felt, but the far greater obstacles to her expression seemed to be lack of time and the sheer amount of work needing to be done. She says in the letters she doesn't have as much time to read as she would like, which must have been deeply frustrating for a woman of her intelligence and desire to learn.

Christopher Grieve's use of language in personal letters can be contrasted with Hugh MacDiarmid's use of language in his poetry. Anyone who has crouched by a dying fire, trying to blow life into the embers, will understand one of MacDiarmid's aims for language in his poetry: to search out dead or dying words from dictionaries, or from other languages, and trying, through inclusion in his work, to breathe life into them once more, that is, to include them in the lexicon to serve the movements of the mind or heart more precisely. In his letters, Christopher Grieve still uses language as a master craftsman, but is now picking up his tools to produce a functional object rather than the virtuoso pieces which will remain as examples of his poetic genius. Valda is much less self-conscious in her use of language, using more idioms (e.g. 'by the bye') and phrases from spoken language, so that one gets the impression she is writing more or less just as she would speak. Christopher's vocabulary and sentence structure in the newly discovered letters (see Appendix IV) are amongst the features that immediately identify them as from Christopher's pen.

The following is one sentence, from MacDiarmid's autobiography. I have selected this particular sentence since it relates to the narrative of Valda and Christopher's life together, but the purpose in quoting it here is to give just a glimpse, through its syntactic complexity, of the thought processes of Valda's husband (see Appendix I). The preceding sentence is simple enough: 'I came to Whalsay, this little north Isle of the Shetland Group, in 1933.' This follows:

> *I was absolutely down-and-out at the time – with no money behind me at all, broken down in health, unable to secure remunerative employment of any kind, and wholly concentrated on projects in poetry and other literary fields which could bring me no monetary return whatever, involved continuous intense effort ridiculously out of proportion to my strength, and called for facilities, in the way of books, papers, and even intercourse – the friction of mind upon mind, since isolation and a too complete self-centredness were definitely dangerous, not*

only to the qualities of the work to be produced but to my own mental stability or, if scarcely that – for if I had been capable of developing any form of insanity, I would certainly have carried myself irrevocably over the border line long ago – at least to the generation and maintenance of the necessary, or at any rate the most helpful, mood.'[9]

How did Valda respond to a man who thought like this? Simply by being herself.

Later in life, Valda published poetry of her own. She had also planned to write a Cornish cookbook – Deirdre Grieve and Norman MacCaig's wife Isabel were helping her with the typing of this. There are also notes for her autobiography to be found amongst her papers.

It seems to annoy deeply some of my generation (poets living in Scotland) that MacDiarmid expressed political opinions or developed political arguments in his poetry. They would like to keep the apolitical lyrics as his 'best' and ditch the rest. Poets whose work is infused with political thought or observation have usually had to lead lives made much more difficult by societal organisation and political events than our own: unlike today, when our Government has engaged the country in perpetual war, yet we can still go down to the local shops and buy more than we will ever need. MacDiarmid's life was directly and intimately affected by two world wars. Such poets live their internal and external lives equally, if not more so, in the social realm as in the private, because historical circumstances have forced them to do so. This situation holds as much today in international terms as it did in MacDiarmid's Scotland. One has only to think of Mahmoud Darwish in military-controlled Ramallah or of any one of the poets living in exile amongst us in Britain today. Would these critics also berate Darwish for writing poetry about identity cards? There is no reason why love in poetry should be limited to the Greek senses of eros, ludus or pragma and not encompass the poet's love for humanity as a whole (*agape*) also. Good poetry expressing political

[9] *Lucky Poet*, p. 41.

opinions is an equally valid form of love poetry. Poems like MacDiarmid's *The Seamless Garment* from *First Hymn to Lenin and Other Poems* (1931) are infused with a great sense of *agape*. The social and political realm is the realm in which MacDiarmid had of necessity to live, for periods, and his poetry is the greater for embracing that. Likewise with Valda's personality: years of struggle do develop in one a pretty good radar for disingenuousness and an intolerance of perceived unkindness. The impression of some who had met Valda, as recounted to me, was of a formidable woman. Some were scared. Hopefully these letters will give a greater depth of understanding and insight into her character than has appeared thus far.

Natural talent or inherited potential needs to be recognised in early childhood and encouraged. Social circumstances contribute to this early nurturance and continue to shape the intellect and creativity throughout life. Examining the principles of justice in a democratic society, one of John Rawls' basic points is that 'native endowments of various kinds (say, native intelligence and natural ability) are not fixed natural assets with a constant capacity. They are merely potential and cannot come to fruition apart from social conditions; and when realized they can take but one or a few of many possible forms. Educated and trained abilities are always a selection, and a small selection at that, from a wide range of possibilities that might have been fulfilled. Among what affects their realization are social attitudes of encouragement and support, and institutions concerned with their early discipline and use… our realized abilities and talents, reflect our personal history, opportunities and social position, and the influence of good and ill fortune.'[10] The young Grieve lad whose family moved into The Library Buildings, where he was allowed to carry down laundry-basket-fulls of books at a time from the well-stocked library upstairs, started out life in hyperlexia heaven. As a young man, Christopher Grieve sensed what he would be unable to do (teaching) and turned to what he knew, choosing in his second wife an ally who would help him achieve his potential. The world of writing, publishing, bookselling was vastly different from what it is today. Generosity of support and communication between intellectuals was vastly different and

[10] pp. 57-8, and reiterated p. 158, John Rawls, *Justice as Fairness*.

has been affected by economic change including competitiveness for small state grants. Can there be any better argument than the struggle to survive revealed here, for a Scottish Aosdána[11] -type affiliation for our arists? These letters reveal a great deal about the changing relationship between writers, readers and society. They also show us how far away we have gone from a culture which can respect and nurture intellect and creativity of Hugh MacDiarmid's quality.

I hope readers of these letters will be inspired to return to or seek out MacDiarmid's poetry and other writing.

Finally, it cannot go unremarked that these letters are part of what is likely to be the last generation of letters that span a whole lifetime. My generation started out with written correspondence, but much communication between writers today is by e-mail, www-sites including poets' web-logs or 'blogs', on-line diaries and by telephone – not in letter form consistently enough through time to provide a complete written dialogue such as this one between Christopher and Valda Grieve. It is precious indeed and a privilege, bestowed by the family's generosity to the wider social group, as well as by their emotional fortitude, to be able to read these. Instead of focusing on the personal (as we are now conditioned to do) we should acknowledge this privilege, by looking for the lessons implicit in Rawls' philosophy. 'Inclusion' is a fine concept but it must be based on justice as fairness for all, *including* the prodigiously gifted, i.e. the young Christopher Grieves of today. For as long as we remain on this path of destruction of the intellectual and creative life of our society, with precedence given to economic considerations, true 'inclusion', justice and fairness will remain a long way off. We have everything we need – nationally. It is time we started enriching the spirit of the country.

Beth Junor

---

[11] In Ireland, members of the Aosdána (there are currently just over 200, of a possible membership of 250) are artists who have produced a distinguished body of work. They receive an annual stipend designed to enable them to devote their time and energies to their creative work (in 2005 this was 12,180 Euros).

Textual Notes

During 13 years of commuting between Edinburgh and the Forth Valley area, the tedium of motorway driving was broken, at times, by the most beautiful natural phenomena. One such reward came an evening in late winter, when I began the last long arch of the M9 that brings the Pentland Hills into view. An afternoon snowfall still lay across their ridges, which between the sky and the dark earth below, appeared as a line of bright Arabic script. The eye was drawn from west to east, seeking some meaning. Looking at Valda Grieve's handwriting is something like that. Not rarely, like that view of the Pentlands, which I never witnessed again, but regularly. By some flight of the imagination, the line of ink on her notepaper may symbolise something. One wants it to symbolise something - in fact, desperately wills it to do so, through the act of staring.

Were it not for the fact I had spent many years – all those days between the commutes – working in language and communication pathology, learning the lesson that an individual's message, no matter how obscured by modes of communication often presenting far denser smokescreens than this, can nevertheless contain a message of surprising interest or importance, I would have taken fright at the first letter I saw and abandoned the whole project.

Should you be irritated by gaps in legibility, please bring to mind the extremely difficult conditions in which Valda was writing, particularly throughout the Shetland years: in the cold and dark, with the fire gone out or with no mantle for the gas lamp, exhausted at the end of a very long day's physical work. Valda herself was conscious of the difficulties her handwriting caused for Christopher; her handwriting difficulties are a recurrent theme throughout her letters. The toddler James Michael has run away with her own pen, or later, it was the 'hellish Biro – it just runs away with you,' and so on. Her handwriting does improve considerably as her living conditions improve. She also refers to an inability to express herself; unlike the handwriting, though, this self-perception is not borne out by the evidence. There is not one false note in the letters and her expressive abilities appear no worse than any writer's attempts to rein in feelings or ideas with language.

Punctuation was quite non-existent, consisting mainly of dashes of varying lengths. I have kept enough of these to give a flavour of style, but I have also added a great many sentence breaks and paragraph breaks (sometimes a particularly long dash seemed to signify a new paragraph).

Some spelling errors were systemic, and I have corrected these (for example, Valda always used 'i' before 'e', as in 'recieved'), for ease of reading, but occasional errors have been left, marked by the Latin 'sic' in square brackets. Errors in syntax (more frequent when Valda was extremely exhausted) are indicated thus as well, again for the sake of accuracy to the original, and in order to preserve the flavour of the writing. Possessive apostrophes were sometimes missing as were contraction apostrophes and I have left these uncorrected, as the sense remains. The interesting thing here is that, given the persistence of errors over the decades, it seems that not once did MacDiarmid draw attention to or correct them – he responded only to the content, fully accepting the form.

Where the handwriting defeated me altogether a question mark appears within square brackets. (This is often used when the marks on the page do not seem to be anything like what you would deduce from the context – so the word is not likely to be simply what your mind will fill in as you read.) Where it has been possible to make a best guess a word appears in square brackets preceded by a question mark. Otherwise, much had to be deduced (particularly names and titles) from what knowledge I did have of MacDiarmid's milieu and writing, as well as from an acquired familiarity with Valda's lexicon and letter formation patterns. Deirdre Grieve and John Manson read the final manuscript and made many helpful suggestions.

Many of the letters are undated and again a lot of contextual detective work went on. This was much easier in the instances in which one could match Valda's letters to Hugh MacDiarmid's published correspondence. Where I have added in dates with certainty, these appear in square brackets. Again, best guesses appear in square brackets prefaced by a question mark.

Where notepaper is torn (as with the first letter in this collection), the tears are marked with square brackets, even where it is quite possible to make a good guess at the missing word(s).

Some writing continues around the edges of the paper (an effort to save paper?) and this is marked in square brackets. All the letters are written on plain paper save a few exceptions when printed headed paper is used, and these exceptions are also indicated, as are telegrams, postcards, letter-cards and airmail letters.

All of the letters have been transcribed in full, except two from which I have left out passages because they intrude upon the privacy of the extended family and another family to an extent I did not feel was justified by the interests of social or literary history. These passages are marked by three dots within square brackets: [...].

I had to limit myself to Valda's letters to Christopher (although she corresponded with many others), with a few exceptions only, for the purpose of filling out the narrative.

Readers may wish to cross-reference with MacDiarmid's *New Selected Letters* (referred to as *NSL* throughout) in particular, to enjoy both sides of the conversation.

The flower motif used throughout the book is of *Prunus pseudo-cerasus*, a species closely related to *Prunus cerasoides rubra*, the Carmine Cherry MacDiarmid refers to in his *Cornish Heroic Song for Valda Trevlyn*:

But ah! now, beloved, it is as when on the Carmine cherry,
A hundred feet high and with a spread
Coinciding with the circumference of the earth,
The ruby-red flowerbuds open, and the whole tree
Bursts into carmine flame, a mass of blossom, stark crimson.

Many thanks to Colin Will, poet and Head Librarian (retired) at the Royal Botanic Gardens Edinburgh, for searching out this illustration for me. Readers may be interested to learn that the other shrub referred to in this stanza, 'smothered with carillons of little brick-red bells/Finely striped with yellow lines;/ That, when the sun shines through them,/ Glow like hot blown glass' is thought by Colin Will and his former colleagues to be *Enkianthus campanulatus*, known to be growing in several Cornish gardens (Trewithen, Boscawne, Trebah) at the time.

Hugh MacDiarmid: New Selected Letters, edited by Dorian Grieve, Owen Dudley Edwards and Alan Riach (Manchester: Carcanet Press, 2001).

Part 1

Cornwall to Shetland

In April 1933 Christopher Grieve wrote to his brother that he would very soon be going "to Shetland for some months to get some new books written..."[12] *– a statement which, with hindsight, must qualify as one of the century's greatest understatements. He arrived on 4th May 1933, to begin one of the most prolific writing periods – certainly in terms of poetry – of his life.*

Although Valda had previously joined Christopher in Scotland from Sussex soon after the birth of their child, here she has returned to Cornwall to stay with her mother and two aunts for approximately two months (in mid-May 1933 Christopher wrote, '...more than half the time of our separation has now passed'[13]*).*

The notepaper of this first of Valda's letters to be preserved is torn and contains on its reverse a poem in Christopher's hand, written to mark the wedding of his host Dr Orr and published in The Free Man *on 27th May 1933 – this poem perhaps being the original reason for preserving the letter, even if it wasn't to remain the sole reason.*

Christopher and Valda's son James Michael is now 9 ½ months old.

---

[12] *NSL*, p. 52.

[13] *NSL*, p. 56.

28, King Street
Bude
Nth Cornwall

13/5/33

[missing, page torn] Christopher,

You're probably thinking all sorts of dreadful things about me – please forget them.

I was frightfully bucked to get your letter – before I was so very worried wondering what had happened to you that it was impossible for me to write, now the only excuse I have to offer is dressmaking and quite an inadequate one to my mind.

The island, the people, in fact everything about the place sounds entrancing – I know I shall love it – and you – mon chere – there is a different sound [*torn section*] … of yours, face things [*torn*] show the whole damned crowd of nit-wits what you can do – you'll be more of a lone wolf then [?*love*] but it's worth it Christopher.

The weather here has not been too good – today it is raining hard. I've managed to invest in a mac & that reminds me – have you written to Michael[14] as I want to settle some of the a/c – for if I do not do so soon I fear I'll spend it all as you already know – I'm not good at holding on to the ha'pence.

Also send me [?] McLeods [?*token*] & Millars receipts, will you.

You had better write + tell Michael not to sell the pillow, blankets etc Pyrex casserole and to send all odd +ends on to us.

Let me hear as soon as you can about it, won't you?

I'm enclosing trunk key – sorry: - the small case is not locked – by the bye do I leave here Monday week or have I to stay longer much as I am enjoying myself I would far rather be with you – for I miss

[14] Appears to have been left in charge of the Grieves' affairs after they hurriedly left Thakeham. His real name was 'A.R. Duy Vinecomt' or 'Vinecomb' (from his own handwriting) - John Manson, corresp.

you terribly on the other hand I do not wish to push myself upon you & Dr Orr before it is quite convenient, sorry!

The housekeeping stint fills me with awe. I'm overwhelmed already at the mere thought of my new responsibilities – How can I – You expect too much. Wash for – cook for – sleep for – (sorry that last bit is all wrong) " a mountain of jollity"[15]. The devil help me! I'll do my best. Kiss him (Dr Orr) chastely upon his noble brow for me, will you – Thanks!

James Michael is doing splendidly – he's more spoilt than ever – my mother thinks I'm heartless & not in the least fit to look after the 'puir little dear' he's too thin – "no stomach on him at all."

He was weighed yesterday 19 lbs. 2oz. So that's that. After a week of feeding like a fighting cock I [?] him the scales – Guess

~ 1 st 13 oz ~ [16]

Where are the Faroe Islands? I haven't had time to look it up - .

The Free Man came today. I was glad to get it - .

Mary Bitchface[17] Margaret Black[18] – Robin Black[19] – have written me – also got my camera from the [?] – it's [*ripping*?] - .

Mother & aunts all send their love to you and as for myself you already have it all.

Valda & James Michael

[15] Valda quotes back this characterisation of Dr Orr from Christopher's letter of 8th May. Christopher had suggested Valda act as housekeeper "(with the help, probably, of a little day girl)" for Dr Orr, in whose house he is staying. From Christopher's descriptions the house seems commodious enough to accommodate himself, Valda and James Michael, in addition to the Dr & his new wife (*NSL*, pp 53-4).

[16] This is perhaps the earlier weight; at 19 lbs. 2 oz. JM was within normal limits for an infant of his age.

[17] Mary Lichfield, who was referred to as Mary Bitchface. She played a social part in writers' lives – knew the Mitchells, the Muirs, the Carswells, the Grieves, et al. and was a Communist Party member. – John Manson, corresp.

[18] Had a laundry in Glasgow.

[19] Robert (Robin) MacKelvie Black, editor and proprietor of *The Free Man*.

Verso of last page [Christopher's handwriting]:

Bedtime [20] (a little epithalamium for David and Margaret Orr,

Broch Schoolhouse,
Island of Whalsay,

May 1933)

She's like a pond in the woods
Destined to lie
Reflectin' a circle o' leaves
And short tract o' sky.

Kennin' nocht o' the vastity
That surroonds and weighs on it,
A' the firmament and the forest;
Where nae ither man can gaze on it.

[20] Published in *The Free Man* 27.5.33. See *Complete Poems, Volume II*, p. 1274.

28, King Street
Bude
Nth Cornwall

[? *Wed. 17 May 1933*]

My dear!

The *Daily Mail* has been devoting a column each day for the past three days[21] to herring fishing [?] the Shetlands Orkneys & the Faroe Islands & pointing out all the dangers etc & the number of boats that have come to grief this year – more than any of the preceding years – have decided no herring fishing for this child. Life is still good & the thought of marble stairs & lamps are not so alluring as to make me want to tempt the Providence.

There are so many things I want to say to you mon cher Christopher – but always seem rushed when I sit down to write – either the post is about to go, or the wee man awakes or – stop or I shall go on ever & ever Amen.

Heaven only knows what we shall do with James Michael for he has developed into an arrogant little trumpet, scarcely sleeps at all during the day, is full of buck & backchat, simply refuses to go to bed at night until about 9pm., won't stay in his cot & when strapped in the pram promptly wriggles over the side & hangs on the strap & yells. This he does deliberately for I've watched him doing it – the little devil – the son of his father believe me.

[21] The *Daily Mail* ('FOR KING AND EMPIRE')'s Montague Smith's series of reports opened with the headline '*DAILY MAIL* INQUIRY INTO FISHING INDUSTRY' on Monday May 15th 1933; Tuesday's article 'HERRING FISHERS' GAMBLE FOR A LIVING' was illustrated with a rather alarming photograph 'A drifter battling home in a rough sea'; Wednesday's was 'NEW MENACE TO BRITISH FISHERIES' ("a systematic attempt by Swedish vessels to capture the market") and so on, 'round the coast; these amidst articles reporting Herr Hitler's activities, South African women voting for the first time, etc. Christopher, himself just back from herring fishing, replied on 27th May, 'Damn the *Daily Mail* and its stupid articles. ...' – *NSL*, p. 60.

The life of Stringberg [*sic*][22] interested me very much & that reminds me I must send it back – last week's *Free Man* was 'no sae bad' but I've read better issues.

Look here! – you adorable bugger how on earth do you think I can cook meals to compare anyway near the menu you enclosed – have you been frank with the Doc & told him all my deficiencies in the domestic way of things. Honestly old dear it is no joke & I'm 'worrit' to death – my hair is becoming more grey than ever & my face lined with wrinkles. Alas alack – ah me – think I better stay on down here & you two mates get a housekeeper - anyway I'll do my best & may the good Lord protect me.

About coming over to you – if I'm to get back on the cheap ticket I'll have to leave Bude on Wednesday 31st – spend a night & day in London with the Johnstons. This means I'll arrive in Edinburgh on the Friday, collect & pack a few things I have at Mrs Tarbruck. The things I'm sending on in advance had I better send them direct to you or if that is impossible where had I better send them to the docks at Leith or what – I'd like to know everything well beforehand & so prevent a rush in the end.

I've paid the Pulborough paper account & have the receipt – have you written to Michael yet for the accounts? Also you'd better tell him not to sell the pillows, blankets etc – my Pyrex casserole & to send on your crayon drawing by A.E.

The house sounds awfully nice – like you I hope we'll be able to stay on for some time. How are managing [*sic*] for dibs? Hope you've dropped Whyte a friendly note – I've sent him a card. All here send their love – they were very pleased with the cards – the post half a sec!

---

[22] *Married. Twenty stories of married life*, by August Strindberg, transl. Ellie Schleussner, had been published in London in 1913. Strindberg married the actor Siri von Essen on the last day of 1877. Siri had been reluctant to marry, fearing that marriage to Strindberg would mean slavery. In 1883-84, Strindberg began work 'on a volume of stories about marriage which exploded chivalry and romance as senseless fantasies, and showed the real relationship between the sexes as a fight based on the instinct of reproduction and the economics of living.... [*Strindberg*] confessed to [*Siri*] that he was writing a diatribe against married life, and begged her, if she read the

5 mins later

Just had a long letter from Mrs Robertson[23] & I gather from her letter & from Robin Black that the Right Wing are going to have it all their own way at the conference curse them!

Are you getting into the guts of the *Frontier* – I shall expect to see stacks of MSS. on my return so work hard laddie.

I'm sending a parcel of odds & ends on to you at the beginning of the week, towels etc etc etc.

Yesterday I had a lovely bathe & will try & get another today if I am finished my sewing up in time. JM is very sunburnt – we'll send on a few snaps the next time –

Kind regards to the Doc

All my love.

Valda

The Bathing Pool, Bude, from a postcard of the period.

stories, to remember that the marriages he described were purely hypothetical, and that the sole aim of his attack was to spur men and women on towards a better relationship, instead of allowing themselves to be fooled by a romantic illusion which could only end in despair.' (pp. 82,95,96, *The Strange Life of August Strindberg*, by Elizabeth Sprigge). Therefore when Valda writes on 22nd May that she is under no delusions where marital things are concerned, she may have had these stories in mind.

[23] Mrs (Nan) Robertson's husband was Stanley Robertson, Musselburgh dentist.

28, King Street
Bude
Sunday

[*c. 21 May 1933*]

Dear Christopher!

If it's half as nice at Whalsay as it is down here – well I'll be satisfied – the last week has been perfect – I'd like to live like this for ever & ever – with you to share it – of course sweetone.

What frivolities have you been indulging in since last I received a missive from you – many moons ago. Did you win the booby prize at the whist drive?

What's happened to the *Selected Poems* – has Gollancz[24] decided to get on with it or has he put it on the 'wait and see' list? Tell me in your next letter.

I'm on the beach trying to write this – my thoughts will go off on the tangents & the sea looks so tempting & I've only had one bathe today & I'd best have another – may I? Thank you darling – but it seems I must finish this letter.

Cheerio

V.

Monday morning
[*22 May 1933*]

This morning I expected to hear from you but - only received a queer note from Mrs Craik[25] reminding me that her husband was still a "something or other" officer (I couldn't make head or tail of it) & that the furniture never turned up – I was under the impression that you had 'phoned Guys -Aberlady up & made all arrangements – apparently other things were occupying your mind. I'm very annoyed

[24] Victor Gollancz had established a publishing firm in Henrietta Street, Covent Garden in 1928. He published Christopher's *Stony Limits and Other Poems* in 1934.

[25] Mrs Craik, Edinburgh, stored furniture from Fruit Farm Cottage, Longniddry, for the Grieves.

about it – after all, Mrs Alexander is waiting to get into the cottage – one would think sometimes that we were the only pebbles on the beach – personally where marital things are concerned I'm under no delusions – anyway I'm writing to them today – so you need not bother to do anything in the matter.[26]

Everyone here sends love to you & hope things are well with you – .

James Michael is looking very fit & full of beans.

If I do not hear the contrary from you I shall catch the boat on Tuesday night June 6th – . My kind regards to Dr Orr.

Sincerely

Valda

[26] 'Sorry to get your snotty little note. I wasn't in the least irresponsible about the furniture...' Christopher replied on 27 May (*NSL* pp60-61), explaining the efforts he'd made to arrange these matters. The other matters occupying his mind included a 900-line poem, 'Ode to all Rebels'; by late May he had also completed 20 or so lyrics, with notes for up to 60 more. (Brian Smith in *MacDiarmid in Shetland*).

28, King Street
Bude
Nth Cornwall
[*between 22-31 May 1933*]

Darling!

I was an awful pig in my last I know – forgive me.

Feeling very excited at the thought of seeing you again - & so full up about the muse – that's the stuff Hugh MacDiarmid.

I hate leaving home – earlier began to get a bit watery eyed etc etc & this damned pen won't write – curse it -

What is your fancy for the Derby - ? I'm not keen on any, but I'm putting a bob on Caymanas and I think Gino.[27]

The cottage[28] still appeals to me far more than the previous arrangements. Will write you or wire you when arriving – I'll catch the boat on Tuesday 6th at Leith and follow your instructions. You'll see an awful change in James Michael – by the bye mother and aunt had him christened last Sunday. I was not there Christopher dear.

I am longing to see you again – to be with you.

All news when we meet – please be in a chatty mood.

Love Valda & JamesM

I'm staying at 8, Westhall Gardens [*Mrs Craik's*] for a few days.

---

[27] The papers had been full of the Derby: 'A nation cannot always be groaning and moaning. It must have some relaxations. And amid the multitude of problems which confront the world, such as war and debts [*payment of war debt instalments to the United States*] and tariffs, what is the subject which is most likely to be discussed wherever men are gathered together in the quiet hours of the week-end? We should be willing to bet it will be the chance of this or that horse for the Derby. ...' said the *Daily Mail* on 27th May 1933. On 30th May, the day before the race, Caymanas (Mr Crum Ewing) was 40-1; Gino (Aga Khan) was 28-1; the 1933 winner was Hyperion (Lord Derby).

[28] Christopher had written with news of securing a cottage for a year. Johnnie Georgie Anderson, skipper of the *Research*, with whom Christopher had sailed for a few days at the herring fishing from 22nd May '33, told Christopher he had a cottage at Sudheim (anglicised as 'Sodom'), in which his son Andrew had died of TB at the age of 21, and which he had vacated only a few months earlier in favour of a house with land attached. – 'After sixty years: once more on the Grieves in Whalsay, 1933-42' by John Manson, in *The New Shetlander* No. 223, 2003, pp. 17-21.

Valda and James Michael arrived in Whalsay on 8th June 1933. Christopher travelled to the Faroe Islands on 26th July; this letter appears to date from a later separation necessitated by Christopher's participation in the Aberdeen University Rectorial election.

Sodom
Thursday 11.15pm

My dear Christopher,

So you came in Third which was jolly good considering all the unpleasant things you must have said.

Many thanks for letter you sound just too respectable – outwardly.

The boat came in this morning & I felt quite disappointed at your not being on - & then to have later received your wire saying you had missed the boat. Miracles happen even in these days it seems. I never thought the day would come when a steamer could travel faster than a telegram – but we live & learn. I am penniless as usual, but Orr will send a few ha'pence on in a day or two, as there isn't a Tuesday's boat you'll not be in desperate hurry. & now to business.

I hope the wire you received today is quite clear. On Monday the following letter arrived from Jarrolds.

"Dear Mr --------

Our mutual friend Mrs J ----- very kindly gave us their offer of your proposed A of E L.[29] Our readers feel that although without the slightest doubt your work would be superlatively well done, there would be made small return for the labour and outlay expended in producing and publishing it. There is of course the possibility of getting an

[29] At this time Christopher was trying to interest publishers in an Anthology of European Literature in translation (without success).

American Publisher sufficiently interested in the proposition to give us an order for an edition in sheets, and although this would help us with the cost of production, the Author's financial returns would on their part of the deal be very small.

Shall I return your synopsis so that you may try some other English Publishers? Or shall I see what can be done in America?
Yours -------
Jarrolds Publisher
H.E. Hale

Today received

Dear Mr --------

I should be glad to hear from you at your convenience in response to my letter of the 7th regarding the synopsis of your proposed A. of E L.

Yours . . .

I've kept the letters in case this should miss you – others are as follows.

(1) H.M. Customs & Excise
GPO Grieve
I've returned some unopened - try Edinburgh

(2) Card from your brother.

(3) Letter [?] Morrison (*Scots Observer*) [*editor*]
saying there will be no need to have the permission of Coia or Boden because they paid for the exclusive rights – also if you were in Edinburgh to let him know as he may try & see you sometime.

(4) Bill from Longniddry.

(5) Letter to you from Nan Robertson (wild & drunken you may be but the thought [?*of*] associating with a [?*lord*] Rector so Nan overcame her prejudice. Poor coot![)]

(6) Letter from Gibson [*Gibbon*] – you'd forgotten the Politicians – wanted more very light newsreel stuff to pepper the graver matter. Send photo for Publicity stuff (but I wired you all that). [30]

The others letters look like private ones but as I'm writing you I'll open them & see – half a sec –

(1) Philippe Mairet
31 Haverstock Hill NW3

"You sent me a review of Dents Biographical Dict.s of Foreign literature, and Orage & I were both duly grateful for the same – you did it, indeed upon a much more magnificent scale than I intended, but all the better of course. In your letter you said that you would be very willing to contribute an article to *Purpose* and that is what I wanted to write to you about.

- delighted to have a contribution from you
- anything upon, say, present movements in Continental literature would be suitable
- but so I believe would anything else you would be likely to send.
Articles of about 2,000 words are the best length for us.
Your writing from the North have interested me greatly. - - -
By the way if you cared to do a descriptive & social study of the Shetlands for *Purpose* it would I believe be appreciated more than anything.
- left request rather late - -
must be in 1st week in December –
send PC. to confirm as I do most enthusiastically want to take advantage of your offer. Yours with best wishes Philippe Mairet
[PS *along side of page*: 'we are also [?] still mostly unsigned']

So far so good – old dear!

(2) The next is from Higgins[31] sending you '*Arable holdings*' no question of cash

[30] This refers to *Scottish Scene* (1934).

[31] F.R. Higgins (1896-1941), Irish poet. *Arable Holdings* was published in Dublin in 1933. More recently, he has been anthologised in Ted Hughes' selection *By Heart: 101 Poems to Remember* (Penguin, 2001) and in Michael Longley's selection *20th Century Irish Poems* (Faber, 2002).

Would like a blunt honest to goodness review from you.
"I've a wild, intoxicated, irregular dissolute novel practically finished – but temporarily held up - "
"I've seen some of your punching prose in the *Freeman*. Where's your Muse? Let her dance or take care she doesn't get frostbitten."
"How is the Lamb of Lomond. (W.J.[32] I mean)"

The letters damn fine, isn't it?

(3) From a RJC Hull[33] – Germany

He's translating Rainer Rilke & would like you to criticise his work as you're the only one etc etc.

(4) From Neil Gunn
nothing worth recording – yes one thing, T.S. Eliot descended on him one night & they had a night of it.

That's all, the rest consist of numerous [?] & "item sentiments."

My dear, I think you could have sent me some papers you must know I'm dying to hear & to know all about the 'bun fight.'
Are you staying with your brother or with R.B.[*Robin Black*]? Helen [*Cruickshank*] & everyone fit?

I've been having an unholy time – run out of peats – got some from Hays – now living in the midden heap. Have had JM in [?] a week with a severe cold & cough – breathing difficult at night – so I've brought his cot downstairs, it's warmer during the night. Was up until 1.45 a.m. one night. Today he seems better.

You'll probably curse this scrawl it is worse than usual – but I've cut my forefinger & have difficulty in holding pen – so forgive me – I'll away now – expect money beginning of week. Watch your self laddie

All luck & love Valda

---

32 Possibly William Jeffrey.

33 Rilke authority.

Sodom
Whalsay
Shetland Island

7/12/33

Dear Christopher,

Many thanks for the P.C. and wires. I am very disappointed at having to wait another week for your return. If the *Free Man* is really on its last legs I cannot see that it necessitates your staying on, laddie – or mon cher is it the flesh & the devil? – good Lord! that has a distinctly Plymouth Brethern [*sic*]flavour – it must have been meant for pious faced Tom MacDonald[34] – whose understanding on that will be greater than yours.

If things are really in such a bad way I am frightfully sorry & sincerely hope something will turn up to save the situation – for what would C. M. Grieve do without his platform? This may seem light and bordering on sarcasm I assure it is not what I intend to convey to you.

I'm enclosing all the correspondence with the exception of - *New Britain* – Sean O'Casey's play – with the compliments of Wm. Mc Elroy[35] & the manuscripts from Hull – Germany, on

.

How did the debate go full of fun & fire?

There is a concert here tomorrow – Lerwick party but I'm afraid I will not be able to go – JM & I are down with colds & wretched coughs – honestly old dear my chest is so sore & raw that every time I cough or breathe deeply it makes me feel quite suicidal.

Christopher – be understanding – only, old dear I will not be able to send any more alms. I must get JM a thick coat & some extra cosy things & we have to live & although Black's position is precarious,

---

[34] Fionn MacColla (1906-1975), novelist, who was brought up in the Plymouth Brethren.

[35] Christopher's first wife Peggy's partner. Alan Bold surmises they met in 1929; they split up in 1935. McElroy had funded the transfer of Sean O'Casey plays from Dublin to London (*NSL*, p. 550).

ours is just as bad. Whoever else suffers JM must not, as you know he's never had any of the nice things people like for their bairns.

By the bye you will [*sic*] forget the Xmas shopping - will you? I'm depending on you to bring them.

JM sends salutations to his godfather & many thanks for [*advert?*] of "Claymore."[36] He's not awfully keen on the name – sounds rather 'suburban.'

My kindest regards to all & sundry & a kick in the pants for Fionn M[*a*]cColla me lad, and for you Christopher Grieve all my love.

Slante

Valda

[36] One of Robin Black's publications (or proposed publications).

In the early Spring of 1934, Christopher, Valda & James Michael went to stay in London, so that Christopher 'could do research and make new deals with publishers and others.'[37] While down South, Valda made a return visit to her family in Cornwall.

Tuesday

[*April, 1934*]

Dearest Christopher,

Received wire on reaching home last night.

Mother has been lying dangerously ill for a fortnight – with <u>clots</u> of blood – she may go all out any moment. I've been up sitting with her all the afternoon – it's pitiful to see her – her hands & arms are smaller than mine - & her breath just comes in quick little pants. She was very pleased to see us – she'd told the aunts that I was coming two days before they received my wire – poor little mother – perhaps it would be just as well – she did go. Here there is such an air hopelessness Aunt Jane is stone deaf and weird than ever - & Agnes is home, helping – someone has to be with mother all the time night & day.

I do hope you have a good time – do take care of yourself.

By the way – I do wish you'd take a day off & finish *Red Scotland* – things here aren't too grand – altho' they haven't said anything – it is very noticeable.

---

[37] Brian Smith in *MacDiarmid in Shetland*, pp 47 ff. 'They arrived in London on 15th March. One of MacDiarmid's immediate aims in coming to London was to bring back the Stone of Destiny to Scotland.... However, MacDiarmid finally concluded that the attempt was too difficult. ... MacDiarmid visited Lewis Grassic Gibbon in Welwyn Garden City either in March or in April. ...Perhaps the most fruitful outcome of these seven months in London was the conception of 'The Red Lion' project' which included poems about Glasgow and 'In the Slums of Glasgow.' – John Manson, 'Hugh MacDiarmid in England (1929-34), in *Markings* 20/21, 2005.

Charles[38] too, is in a bad way – he managed to get the cheque changed for me – so do be careful & don't overdraw your a/c. I bought [*Beatrice*] Hastings[39] – pamphlet on Orage (about her at [?]) have got the *Left Review* – also – *The Life of Herbert Henry Asquith* – 2 Vol. & "*Your Frightened People*" – Penguin series. Will send them on to you at the end of the week – by the way – don't lose my D.H. Lawrence which is in your overcoat pocket – looking forward to hearing from you – forgive my selfishness darling – for I don't suppose you will have much spare time – hope the painting goes off O.K. ______________ My kindest regards ________ to the Barker-Fairley's & all love to yourself

Valda

[38] Likely Charles Lahr.

[39] see 'To My Friend the Late Beatrice Hastings' (in Fyfield Books/Carcanet's *Selected Poetry*).

28, King Street
Bude
Nth Cornwall

21/4/34

My dear Christopher,

How are things? I received the *Five Bits of Miller* – Old Aunt Jane started reading it with aid of spectacles & a magnifying glass. She managed to get as far as the "ear part" & was then violently sick. She has definitely come to the conclusion that you're mad. I hope you received my wire in good time. I'm very worried about it – as Johnnie Georgie[40] did not sound too sweet. What have you done about it? You will do something won't you quickly. I wrote & said that you'd be back in about a fortnight – but the letter will take a week to get there. Please let me know all news & what you have done in this matter – for you must realise it vitally concerns us our being together –

May I have a letter quite soon

Love

Valda

P.S.

Sent to Selfridges today for some bargains for the cottage – I'm now broke to the wire – S.O.S.

[40] Anderson, owner, at the time, of the cottage at Sudheim (Sodom) – which Christopher is in the process of purchasing.

Dear C

In a hurry to catch the post – have repaired my grey flannel trousers for you – I think the buttons are put in correctly – if not – no doubt Mrs Scott will alter them for you.

Received your letter this morning - & I'm glad you're back in Scotland again. I had heard of your departure & that McElroy & Mrs Grieve saw you off.

I hope you'll be able to settle the cottage quite soon – do not forget to let me know in good time otherwise there will not be any clothes for you to sleep in – also about your other things – have you taken everything from the Carswell's to the Hotel – if you let me know I'll get them for you – also my shoes.

My aunt is returning on Monday – she is still in a very weak condition.

We are having very miscellaneous weather – yesterday was a scorcher & today hailstones.

James Michael is very fit & full of beans & sends you love & kisses – he still talks of you.

My kindest regards to Mrs Scott & F.G[41].

Sincerely
Valda

Will send some cream at the beginning of week.

[41] F.G.Scott (1880-1958), composer whose collaboration with MacDiarmid is said to have been central to his development as a song-writer (see *Songs of FG Scott*, by Neil Mackay). Scott wrote settings for *The Watergaw*, *Crowdieknowe* and *The Eemis Stane*, from MacDiarmid's 1925 collection *Sangschaw*. Christopher later stayed with the Scotts in Glasgow during the War, when the Scotts received many of the parcels of papers, manuscripts, etc. Valda sent; Valda endeavoured to find some scarce wool for Mrs Scott during these years and seems to have corresponded with her about this (see below).

28, King Street
Bude
Nth Cornwall

30/4/34

Dear Christopher,

Received your letter this middle day – sorry to hear things are so bad with financially [*sic*] – it is the same this end.

Have just wired you £1. which I had to borrow from Mrs Fellowes. If you have managed to raise any I would like it back, as I'm absolutely penniless it is very humiliating to have to ask one's mother for money to buy a stamp with.

The weather is wonderful. JM has been on the beach this morning without any clothes – he sends you his love.

Hope to hear better news ere long.

Yours Sincerely

Valda Trevlyn

10/5/34

My dear C

What about it – do you think it possible to raise the "dough" or half of it. This cottage[42] stands by itself about 6 miles from Bude. You know the bungalows at Widemouth there looks so rotten all in a row – well – you turn off just there & it's up a lane – there is a kitchen & sitting room with tiled floor – two bedroom – well just outside the door & a small garden. I'm getting up early tomorrow & going to see it.

If it is sensible I'd like it so much better than Shetland - see the sunshine we should have it's nearer London too.

About the Shetland place you could easily say that I've had an examination by a Dr & he advises me not to go back – bad for my chest etc etc. .

Almost forgotten there are some rates to pay per year – 32S – the cottage is Freehold.

No more until tomorrow – when I've seen it I may not be so enthusiastic.

Cheerio. V.

11.40 A.M.

Have just come back – got up early & walked out to see the place. Christopher it is ideal. I don't know where to start first.

It's really isolated – but within easy reach of the main road to the sea. It's in a lane off the main road (10 mins) & ¼ hour from Widemouth beach.

Whitewashed & thatched – a really nice sitting room quite a decent size (about the size of our kitchen here & sitting though into one) floor covered with small red tiles. Usual kitchen with adorable little cubby-holes. Wash-house with copper for boiling clothes – and a well (this needs a deeper collar – otherwise OK).

---

42 Christopher had asked Valda to look out for a cottage in Cornwall they could rent for a few months.

A nice flower garden full of polanthums (can't spell it) & wall flowers a good size triangular vegetable garden.

The whole thing could easily be made bigger when we have the money. 1 double size bedroom & one small.

I went to see the owner today. She seemed very nice. I explained to her that we could not afford £200 for it all at once – so she said that she would be only too glad to meet us. I suggested £50 down & another £50 end of year & next year the same. She was quite agreeable.

Do lets get it – it's truly worth the money - & I'd love it – it's out of Bude too – but within easy reach. We could dump JM with mother at any time – grow our own lettuce, turnips & carrots – have [?*stocks*] & [?*marguerite*] in the garden improve the cottage when we can afford it – it's freehold.

We could hike in the summer & be able to leave JM with Mum – or if we wanted a weekend to ourselves.

We could easily have a sectional hut put in the garden with a bed in it for anyone staying with us.

Write me soon please & it won't be standing soon – these sort of chances do not come twice – it will really be our own if anything happened to you & one never knows I could always live there whereas I couldn't in Shetland.

It would be easy to get rid of Anderson tell him he could have the stove as compensation sell the other stuff - & these would help to pay off things & Mrs Nicholson.[43] The wooden box & books Dr Orr could pack up in the tea boxes. Did your mother leave you anything?

Christopher you will get this tomorrow do write me immediately <u>do do</u> try to get the place – know you would like it. Mother would give

[43] Mrs Jemima Nicolson, Whalsay postmistress.

me a few odd things & it wouldn't take much to furnish it. Get the money from somewhere. Do! Do! Do! I've never wanted anything so badly in all my life.

Bargains like that soon get picked up.

This calls for love I think – so here goes

All my Love

Valda

In my excitement have rather muddled the pages –

Sorry!

V.

28, King Street
Bude

[*May 1934*]

Dear C

Many thanks for letter received yesterday – so sorry I cannot help you, even with a little – I'm in the same boat myself – have to ask Mum for 1½ for a stamp etc etc – if my P Office Saving book turned up it would be alright – but it hasn't. I wrote to Mrs Nicholson about it & she said it was sent to your London address quite soon after we left Whalsay. I cannot for the life of me think what has happened – because it has not been returned to her. Could you write & ask Nancy ?

How about the house – I've rather a disappointment for you – I honestly think the rooms are too small – from the outside it looks & is adorable & the other morning when I walked up the person was out who live in it & I had to peer through the window & so had no idea really of the size except what the owner said & of course my imagination ran away with me. Listen, carefully the bedrooms are small – one is large enough for a double bed – but the ceilings are very slanting & the walls bulge out so that one couldn't get a wardrobe in (but that doesn't matter) the other a small single room that would just do for JM – the downstairs is the disappointment. I thought there were two rooms & a wash-house – but was mistaken – there is a nicely tiled room – small with a range in it & the smaller room has a copper in it & enough room to keep a few cupboards for saucepans & etc etc.

Now it's not big enough for you to write in – the only other thing would be to have a wooden studio & a couple of bedrooms erected in the garden – you can buy them all ready made in sections – these are quite strong and weatherproof - & very cheap & would not be very expensive to put up. I don't know quite what to do – it's in a lovely spot & I know you'd love it but it would be absolutely necessary to have the other place put up. I was wondering whether if you managed to realise the "shares"[44] & if you had sufficient coming from your mother – whether we could buy this cottage & let the person stay on in it – get the well repaired (I'll try & get the owner to do this) & get the Shetland place – stay there the winter – it's cheaper living about January put it up for sale. I would then be able to pack up things as they should be - & nothing would be lost or things we didn't want packed or would you rather go back & let the place go. I expect we'd be able to find something else another time. I wish you'd discuss it with someone. One thing we'd need is a minimum amount of furniture because there isn't any room for more. I wish to God you could see it! It's lovely it's secluded & yet only ten minutes from the P. Office but we should <u>have</u> to <u>have</u> the <u>other place</u> put up - - so don't do anything about the Whalsay place until you hear from – let me what [*sic*] you think of it now you've read all this – do you think it would be wiser to stick to Shetland for a couple of years until we are in a more settled position perhaps it would be wiser – what do you think?

Yours aye

Valda

PS
Regards Armstrong's[45] letter – it was opened down side so I read it – why not tell him to send all clothes & bedding (ask about pillows) to here so that they could be cleaned well – they'll need it - & to pack all letters books & bills etc into as little space as possible & to send on my leather suitcase – to wherever we intend to be – perhaps we'd better go back it will be cheaper. & we'd better do it quickly 'cos I'll not be able to stay here much longer.

Have just been interviewing the builder.

It'll cost £100 just to strengthen the wall & have studio put in the garden so it's not worth it – so we'll stick to our original idea – sorry to have bothered you so – glad to hear about Macmillan – hope you'll have luck with the shares.

---

44 The "shares" were in the Unicorn Press.

45 J.R. Armstrong, in whose garage in Storrington the Grieves' effects were stored – some were still there in 1940.

Bude

[*May 1934*]

My Dear C.

I hear you are in Edinburgh – I'm damnably sorry to hear the *Free Man* has sunk at last – Robin B will be dreadfully down in the dumps I expect. What's going to be done about it?

Now for goodness sake be sensible – if your money should come through – think of your strong child & its mother – this is considered a melodrama in all third class plays I believe. Joking apart – do settle up from Sodom as soon as you get it – otherwise it will all go the same way. Also I owe Mrs Nicholson £4-6 – 0 & Hays

£3-15-6. I don't want to come back & have old debts to settle.

I had a letter from Janet Irvine this morning Maguire wants to know if you still want the peats cut – as there is a rumour going round that we're not coming back – they hope we are.

Mrs G_____ sends N___ love – as the cottage is no good we'd better [?*jeb*] Sodom & square up for it quickly – so let me know & I'll write to Janet early next week & can then tell Maguire to get on with the peats.

I had a good mail yesterday – amongst it a very nice letter from Whyte.[46] It's Whitsun this weekend would you please send me some money. You must have a little or else you couldn't have got to Edinburgh. If it's only £1 or bulk of I'll be glad. By the way when are we going back in? It is impossible for me to stay here much after June 9th – it's not fair on my people. My aunt is very ill indeed & now that she is home it's more than they can manage – they even have to supply me with pocket money. No wonder they think it's a bit stiff. You'll get my letter today explaining about the cottage if we have to spend all that on repairs it really isn't worth it.

So settle up for the cottage in Whalsay as soon as you get some money – otherwise we will have nowhere to go.

[46] J.H. Whyte, editor of *The Modern Scot.*

What are you doing about the Congress are you staying for that – I hear that they have not got much more than half of the £5000 [*£50.00*] needed for it. Bet poor Helen is worried also that a stinker[47] of yours is appearing in the *Modern Scott* [*sic*].

+ have you heard anything about the "*Five Bits of Miller*"?

When is *Scottish Scene* coming out? - also *Stony Limits* - ? Surely they should be out by now?

There are several things here for Whitsun: Boxing matches, dances – special programme at the P.H., Garden Fete, dancing on the lawn etc etc & the hunt – I'm going to the latter as it's free – the others, unless some dough comes in I'll have to forgo.

Did the cream arrive OK that I sent.

As soon as you've decided to get back to Whalsay let me know – then I can send the bed clothes on.

Yours sincerely
Valda

[47] The 'stinker' was 'Welcome to the PEN delegates', published in *The Modern Scot* Vol. V, No.s 1-2, July 1934. See *Complete Poems*, 1299-1302.

Bude
8/7/34

1.50 a.m.

Christopher-

I do think you're behaving very mean – there are quite a lot of letters here – where shall I send them – have you left London or not – Bah! You make me feel sick – you talk of being fond of me – it seems it just when it suits your convenience.

You have probably had a letter from Mrs Henson – one came here today – seeing it was from Thakeham I opened it. She saw your book advertisings in the *Sunday Despatch* & hopes it a good seller so that you can pay her the £5 – what in the bloody hell does this mean. I put most of the money toward that myself – we also had the receipt from that – who's playing up? I answered it right away – said –

The letter came rather as a shock, that before we paid Grant[48] he said you had MSS – you said Michael had taken them all, that we had letter & receipt form Grant, "that either Grant or Mrs Henson was not playing the game & that it was hard to believe it of either of them."

This is just the gist of what I said.

I haven't received your book (Jarrold's) yet – any old time will do I suppose.[49]

---

48 J. Lionel Grant, author of *Male and Female* (1933).

49 Jarrolds published *Scottish Scene* (1934). Christopher replied the advance copies of his books must have all gone to Shetland; he couldn't afford to buy other copies and if he could, anyway, he couldn't afford to post them. Grant had been given the money owed to Mrs Henson, but must have forged the receipt, Christopher thought, and promised to deal with this too (*NSL*, pp. 74-5).

Of course my people think it very queer you do not write. You make it hard for me with them & seeing that you are not sending me any money. You could try & make it easier for me. I'm fed up to the teeth with everything. Life isn't worth living in my opinion – if only I had the pluck – suicide would be an easy way out – just swim out & out – beautiful blue sea – the sun shining – can go no farther – arms up – a few gurgles - & all is over – it sounds so easy

but —

Valda

28 King Street
Bude

Thursday

My dear Christopher,

Thank you for your letter – I have quite recovered from my hysterical mood – it is so weak to give way to these sort of things.

How are things going with you – not too satisfactory I presume or else I should have heard something. How much longer are you going to stay in London? I saw a small piece in a back number of the *Daily Express* May about the libel action & that Bastard had withdrawn *Broken Records*[50] – does that mean now they have taken out the passage you objected to (what was it – you have never told me although I've asked many a time) that the "action" does not go on?

Compton Mackenzie reviewed "Scottish Scene" on Tuesday in his best come-to-Sunday-school Daily Mailish manner.[51]

Today came a whole heap of leaflets from Jarrolds – if you give me the names of the various people & the necessary £. S. D. I'll post them from here, if you like.

Also the enclosed from Plymouth – I saw the postmark & something sort of told me what it was, so I opened it. What are you going to do about it – will you write to *The Criterion* & explain that you received no payment for the *Second Hymn to Lenin* – or did you? Perhaps Mrs Grieve received it. Anyway here's the bill & it will have to be settled somewhere or other.

What is happening about the PEN Congress – has it started yet? Are you going?

---

[50] *Broken Record* (1934) by South African writer Roy Campbell; a reference to Christopher was withdrawn before publication. (A rather glowing review had appeared in the *Daily Express* 24th May 1934, in which the reviewer James Agate wrote '....But the main purpose of this book is not aesthetic charm, or anything like it. "Broken Record" is a smashing attack on the life contemplative in so far as that life is smug, and a gay, high-spirited championship of life on horse-back, in the open air, preferably on some dangerous quest.')

[51] The column 'Compton Mackenzie on the Week's Books' appeared weekly in the *Daily Mail.*

Have you tried to get someone to take a mortgage for the house yet – surely someone wouldn't mind risking a paltry £55- .

About Grant have you written him yet – or are you still broke to the wire? I wonder – or are you just letting things slide. If things are going on indefinitely like this, I'll have to come up to London & try & get some employment of some sort – it's simply hellish being down here without a penny in one's pocket & nothing to do. I'm bored to distraction.

My aunt [*Jane*] I'm afraid will have to give up Miss Prescotts – she is not strong enough even to supervise things, so that will be another addition to No. 28, all woman-wit in a bed – Christ it make[*s*] me feel sick to think of it. I can't & won't stay here much longer. Surely you can make a tremendous effort & let's all get back to Shetland. Anderson's place is quite big enough for us to manage at the moment. What happened about the Unicorn Shares – did Mr Hunt M.P. bite?

Today it is raining hard – the first we've had for about 6 weeks – it is good to see it & feel it.

Cannot you send one change of underclothing & a shirt home here - & I'll let you have it per return.

Had a letter from Chubby today. She said she saw your photo in the *Daily Express* & an article by you.

May I expect a letter from you soon.

Yours sincerely

Valda

Bude
Nth Cornwall

My dear C.

Received your letter this morning + the £1 yesterday thanks very much. What on earth has Roy Campbell said? Or is this just a stunt to get more money? I doubt it.

How are we managing to get the wherewithal to exist in London?

About Shetland. Have you squared off for the cottage yet? I wish you'd make haste & get back because I have to get back there soon. After next year we must try & get a cottage down around here – for I do love it so – so much better than Shetland where I'm an alien. The North is never kind to people from the South. We could then live our own lives – you would find the atmosphere congenial for your work & I could enjoy myself in my own way.

About the peats – shall I tell Maguire to cut them I wrote to you about it before but you never mentioned it. Practically all the others are cut.

By the way I've been making enquiries about my P. Office Saving Book – I wish you'd be truthful for once & tell me whether you've had it or not – or done anything with it. It hurts me to ask you like this, but you let me down before in this way. Then I have no chance – I have always been perfectly frank with you. I'm learning a lot lately – Christopher – you're the teacher – is it for better or worse. I dare not look too deeply into it.

How I long for laughter & sunshine & with it a deep feeling of Peace. The enclosed poems came on Monday – I did not forward them as I was not sure of your address.

Surely your mother's affairs are taking a long time – I had no idea these sort of things were so lengthy unless of course it happened to some very large estate. "One lives & learns" is a very old and true adage.

My kind regards to Gawsworth[52] & any of the crowd when you see them.

My aunts ain't too sweet – I do not want any more cause for unpleasantness. I'm tired of being hurt from one or another of the only people who mean anything to me – you – my aunts – I took JM is the hairdressers today & had his hair cut he looks a real man now. Please write soon & tell me all news.

Love

Valda

P.S. There is a cheap excursion to Bristol on Thursday – I would like to go – so if you have any spare dibs lovey in the week – pass 'em on otherwise I'll not be able to go.

[52] John Gawsworth (1912-1970), poet; the Gawsworths put Christopher up while he was in London. A couple of replies to Valda's letters from this period had come from hotels in London but Christopher flitted from one leaving his luggage and papers behind, because he had no money. He spent a couple of nights in the open, one in Trafalgar Square. Christopher dedicated 'The Little White Rose' to John Gawsworth.

28, King Street
Bude
Nth Cornwall
Wed. 2.30 pm

My dear Christopher,

Received your letter this lunch hour.

If you really got the money order, why did you not enclose it with your letter – it has not come yet – naturally I rushed around & got everything ready to go on the Monday. I had made arrangements to Hunt on the Monday. The hounds meet at Bude on Whit Monday & I had to cancel it. It's years since I've been & I was looking forward to it greatly. I think you could have been a bit more careful also I have not had any cigarettes for the last fortnight. You could have sent me a little – even /of would be acceptable. I think you're behaving very "mean" toward me.

My aunts aren't being very sweet – I don't blame them – I even have to ask them for 1½ d. for a stamp as I've told you before.

Things are most unpleasant here & I shall be glad to get away. You'll get this in the morning so please send me some money & say whether I'm to come up or not.

You were not very explicit in your letter & I could scarcely read it. I gather that a libel action is taking place & that you are as optimistic & sanguine as ever.

Who is it – you did not say – or the whys & wherefores.

I should like to know.
Will expect a wire from early tomorrow (Thursday) so do not fail me.

Good luck.

Valda

28, King Street
Bude
Nth Cornwall

Wed. eve

Dear C.M.

Many thanks for the £2 – so you managed to "raise the wind" – good for you. How much longer are you staying in town? When you do leave please let me know, otherwise it will be impossible for me to get the "bedding" up in time for your arrival. I presume you will go up by bus ~ .

By the way I asked you about my shoes – I left them in the office of the "Northumberland". When you collect the things from Cathie Carswell's why not pack up your dirty clothes, also your grey (2 prs) flannel trousers & I will get them cleaned once here. Please look after your things & do not throw things away just because you haven't room to pack them. In any stationers you can get a sheet of brown paper & some string for 2d. Don't you bother to get the chairs – I've seen some they are just the thing & can get them sent on carriage paid – when I get the money.

'Fraid there is not anything in the way of news to tell. The weather is perfect – we're both getting quite sunburnt. I hope you're feeling well & enjoying yourself.

Have you screwed the *New Britain* people down to something.[53] I think you are exceedingly foolish if you do not do that.

How are the affairs of your wife progressing? Reasonably well I hope & not as bad as you all expected.

My aunt is coming home next week & I'm not quite sure what to do.

[53] Christopher had contributed from October 1933-March 1934 (*NSL*, pp. 77-8).

Perhaps Dr Orr would advance part of "doings" for the cottage or perhaps I could write to Whyte. We haven't had anything from him for some time now – at least not to my knowledge. Of course you may have – I don't know.

Anyway write soon & let me know your plans – the best of luck.

Valda

Thursday noon

Received wire this morning – will send on my shoes - & your trousers – or if you've left anything behind let me know & I'll retrieve it.
– V.

28, King Street
Bude
Nth Cornwall

Wed. eve

Dear Christopher,

Your letter came this morning. I was away before the post came – went to a Hunt & had to get there by 9 a.m. This won't be any further forward if I do wire it, as it's 10 to 1 you'll not be at the address at this time of day – closing time isn't until 11 p.m., is it.

I've enclosed 30/ that is all I can do, it leaves me with just over 10/ - yes! The cheque came yesterday – I wouldn't have opened it only it looked like a bill or notice from the Railway & it was dated back to an early date in May – so thought it wise to open it. It was. Also read the letter. Like Watson Thompson I hesitated whether I should forward it to Mrs Grieve or hang on to it. I paid a few bills I owed at the shops here, paid back Midge 10/ I borrowed when in London & gave my mother 30/ that I had borrowed from her – 30/ I am sending to you - & that's that.

Had a small note from Scott[54], asking me to give you the enclosed – he did not know your address.

On Friday night I'm going up to Poughill to stay for a fortnight – Miss Prescott is going away & she's let my aunt have the place for that time & I could go as well. So after Friday send any letters to:
Coombe Rise
Poughill
Nr Bude
Nth Cornwall

I shan't be down to Bude every day. I hope the case will come off OK.

No! I have not heard anything from your brother.

[54] F.G.Scott (1880-1958), again. (see p. 21).

Fancy meeting Bertie. Give my kind regards to Gawsworth. Do you see anything of Speirs[55] & the dark tanned laddie that lived Paddington way.

The books have not come on yet. Why didn't you inform Jarrolds – you were in London & then they need not have been sent on. Anyway let me know what has to be done & I'll do it. Let me know all news.

Cheerio.

Yours sincerely

Valda

55 Christopher later wrote to F.G. Scott: 'I see advertised in *Times Literary Supplement* a book on the *Scots Literary Tradition* by John Spiers (Chatto and Windus 7/6). I haven't seen it yet but it may be good. It claims to cover the whole field up to today. I knew Spiers in London. He's an Aberdeen man; Cambridge graduate – one of Leavis's group – subsequently Lecturer in Latvia.' – *NSL*, p. 184 (13 July 1940).

Coombe Rise
Poughill
Nr Bude
Wednesday 12 June 1934

Dear Christopher,

How are things going on? Is the case through yet? & when are you going back? In your last letter you said you had bought Mrs Crosskey's[56] house – I thought the Dr had bought it. Have you really bought it, or is it just another of your high-flown tales — ? If so – what have you said to Anderson.

You would like the house I'm staying in – a lovely garden – with a pond full of goldfish – lovely rooms with large windows – I'm trying to write this in bed, but I'm awfully tired have had two strenuous days – on Friday I went otter hunting & yesterday to a badger hunt - I had the pack & one of the huntsmen is taking me to see some fox-cubs.

On Thursday I'm going to the cattle Exhibition – & on Friday to a hunt at Bridgerule. I'll have to be up in time to catch the 7.15 a.m. train – hoping the Good Lord wake me.

No I did not go on the trip I wrote you about – after sending you the 30/ – the exchequer could not stand it – needless to say, I was disappointed, but I am getting used to it now.

By the bye I have had no money from your brother yet – a letter came from him (as it black edged I presume it is) the other day. Will try to remember to send it on tomorrow, it's been knocking about in my bag for a few days. Will leave this until tomorrow post time – there may be a letter from you.

Sincerely
Valda

[56] Mrs Betty Croskey ('Auntie Betty') let out rooms from Anchor Cottage, where Christopher stayed on first arrival, before moving to Dr Orr's house – John Manson, 'After sixty years: once more on the Grieves in Whalsay, 1933-42' in *The New Shetlander*, No. 233, 2003.

28, King Street
Bude
Cornwall

Dear C.

Received your letter this morning – my dear don't be pathetic. It doesn't ring true – about not writing I wasn't alluding to the last few days when quite conceivably you may be short – you ought to know by this time that there is no need to tell fibs to me. Your brother is still anxious for the receipt for £5 sent you on May 22nd. You'd better send it to him.

Fortunately I did not build much hope of Mrs Crosskeys it sounded too good to be true. I do not see much use in getting a cottage for a couple of months down here – for one thing they are so expensive at this time of the year – they want about 2 – 2½ guineas per week.

It is much wiser & better for us to get right back to Shetland.

What about the "libel action" you were building such hopes on? As you did not mention it in your letter as a likely source of income – I presume it is a "dead hole."

Why you came down to London again is beyond me.

I am glad Jack McElroy was acquitted – & so I expect is Mrs Grieve – it is a ghastly thing to see one's luxuries, comforts etc etc – no more.

This wonderful weather is still holding out. Just days & days of glorious hot sunshine.

By the bye who is the Miss or Mrs Reynolds? She intrigues me.

I had a letter from Mrs Henson today. I'm enclosing it. For Goodness try & keep sober when you get some money & see Grant.

JM is well. He's found a photograph of you today – came out hugging it very proudly & informed us excitably "That's Daddy! That's Daddy!"

I'll enclose a stamped envelope so that you will be able to let me know your plans. I hate – Christ only knows it – to ask you about money but please let me have some as soon as you get a windfall.

Give my love to the Gawsworths they are being very decent aren't they – or are you only using it as a "box-office".

This pen is about the awfullest thing I've struck for a long time.

Had a letter from Midge the other day[57] said met you – you were with an awfully nice man & a woman who wasn't much. If you meet her – do offer her drink. She's a nice kid.

Please do make plans for us to get back soon.

I thought "[?]" was due out in July.

JM sends his love – he's just awakened.

Sincerely

Valda

57 'Can't understand reference to Midge – have not seen her to my knowledge – wouldn't know her in any case unless she told me who she was,' Christopher replied (*NSL*, p. 76).

Christopher addressed a meeting 'packed of staff and students to talk about his poetry' at Manchester University on 10th May 1935, on the invitation of Professor Barker Fairley.[58] *He needed to 'get [his] eyes seen to in Edinburgh'*[59] *before returning to Sodom, and stayed overnight in the poet Helen Cruickshank's attic bedroom, known as 'the Prophet's Chamber.'*

1.30 a.m.

15/5/35

Dearest Christopher,

Received your letter today – awfully glad everything went off alright. "Like through Derbyshire" sounds delightful & just what you need.

I'm enclosing one or two letters that came for you. The one from Dents I've answered giving your permission – but saying nothing about the dates – although I felt strongly tempted to do so. Sent a wee note to Pat[60] saying I thought you'd get the typescript in by the end of May (my writing was a good deal better than this – ever been had?).

Stayed at the Manse for the weekend – had a most restful time. The Dr put his foot in it – am learning that the lawyer was called in to find out what had been done with various houses. He stayed up all night pacing the room & as soon as the shop opened went down & accused Baety [*sic*] of being Alpha – call him all the mean skunks & several other things besides. "You won't get a chance to put me away – I stay just long enough to put my affairs in order & then I'm going."

"In future I go into the peoples houses as their Dr – not as a friend" etc etc

---

58 It was here that MacDiarmid first met the artist Barbara Niven – the beginning of a friendship which lasted until her death in 1972, and 'one of the warmest of his life,' John Manson notes (*The New Shetlander*, ibid, pp. 19-20).

59 *NSL*, p. 95

60 AJB Paterson, Sales Manager of Routledge Publishers.

Isn't it unexpected? I never thought he'd get all hot & bothered – did you? The people's attitude is – "When we start on him – then it's time enough for the shoot-out this week."

Awfully pleased you spent the night with Helen – I expect you saw Edwin Muir's article in the *Scotsman* – he gave you a pat on the back.[61]

The weather is dreadful, blowing a gale, snow & freezing hard.

Don't forget the ducks for JM – he's building on them. Now dear one I must away can scarcely keep my eyes open -

All love

Valda

Kindest regards to Mr & Mrs Scott - do try & persuade F.G. to come up here later on.

[61] Muir later (1936) denigrated the use of Scots as a literary language and criticised MacDiarmid's use of it; MacDiarmid became like the proverbial dog with a bone in everything he wrote about Muir henceforth. John Manson recently found the original articles in this debate (from *The Bulletin* January 1938), which readers can find reproduced in the Spring 2005 issue of *Scottish Studies Review*. My thanks to John Manson for providing me with a copy of this. MacDiarmid refers to this initial praise in his first article.

The next separation of Valda and Christopher was in the autumn of 1935.

Christopher's time in London had borne fruit just at the very last, when he secured a contract with Routledge, plus a retainer to introduce to them new Scottish authors; he had contracted to produce four books by the end of March, and by the time he went down to Manchester to give his talk, he was saying he was badly in need of a break, that he was considerably run down and needing a change.

Sorley MacLean visited the family at the end of July and the day after MacLean left, Christopher collapsed with complete nervous exhaustion. Brian Smith has noted, 'Grieve's biographers ... speak about his 'breakdown' as if it were a bolt from the blue in August 1935. But there is ample evidence that his nervous illness developed slowly and insidiously over a long period, and that it had economic as well as emotional roots.'[62]

Dr Orr sent Christopher to The Gilgal, a hospital near Perth (see Appendix III), to recuperate. Valda accompanied him on the journey and returned to Shetland once he began to show signs of recovery. This letter implies James Michael stayed on the island; it is possible he was cared for by the Grieves' neighbour, Harriet Arthur.

The Gilgal Hospital, as it appeared in The One Hundred and Tenth Annual Report of James Murray's Royal Asylum, Perth (Perth: J. Young & Sons, 1937).

[62] *MacDiarmid in Shetland*, ibid, p. 48.

Isle of Whalsay
Shetland Isles

1/9/35

My dear Christopher,

How are you getting on? Everything back here seems so different without you. I hate it like Hell.

There is a letter here for you from John Frazer [*Fraser*] & a book from Sam [*Sorley*] M[*a*]cLean – I have not sent them on as I don't suppose you'll want to be bothered with them – you may rest assured I'll send on any letters that I know will interest you. Now I want you to be as helpful as you possibly can & not as soon as you feel a little better have a spurt of letter-writing. I think it best that you wrote to no-one at all. [*illegible*] It's the only way as far as I can see – it doesn't matter so much about The Gilgal I suppose – but still I'd lay (or lie) low from the start if I were you.

As soon as I can clear things up here – will take JM down to Cornwall & by hook or by crook try & stay near you. I sometimes wish I did not care for you so much. Everything – the Past , Present, & the Future would be so much easier.

James Michael was very pleased to see me back – he seems to have grown quite a bit. He immediately asked for you & to my surprise burst into tears when I told him you were staying away. "Me want my Daddy" – poor little scone he is awfully fond of you. Sometimes I think you forget he's your child as well as mine – there are times when I hardly know what to think. God! What good does it do – I'm a square peg in a round hole alright!

Orr is looking very fit & so is Robin. He's been up for a week, you know. What a height – rather good looking too!

Had a dreadful journey up – very rough & as usual frightfully sea-sick – arrived feeling like nothing on earth.

Will write you again sometime during the week. What is your latest bulletin?

All my love, Valda

To William Aitken

Isle of Whalsay
Shetland Isles

[*9* September *1935*]

Dear Mr Aitken,

— Mr Grieve is seriously [*ill*] & in a Nursing Home — I am sending your letter on to —

F.G Scott Esq.
44, Munro Road
Jordanhill, Glasgow

He will probably be able to give Mr Hood the necessary introductions.

In any case he will be visiting Mr Grieve & if he thinks he is sufficiently strong enough will give him the letter—. Mr Grieve is suffering from "complete nervous exhaustion" — the Dr thinks it will [*be*] quite 2 or 3 months - perhaps longer before he is anything like fit again.

Sorry I cannot help you in this matter.

My kindest regards —

Yours sincerely

Valda Grieve

Isle of Whalsay
Tuesday Evening
[*10 September 1935*]

My dear Christopher,

How awfully glad I was to get your letter, but so sorry you've had such a wretched week – poor darling. I do hope you'll soon be better. I hear the news is fairly satisfactory – a general infection – which can be cured with arsenic/injections[63].

I note you said the Dr could not tell when you contracted it. I hardly expected him to do that – did you? You're the only person, old dear who can have a rough sort of idea of that. Why don't you speak up – it would certainly give Dr Chambers a better idea of things – every little helps in these matters, you know. Quite frankly I think you knew about it & that Peggy did also – otherwise it seems very strange that two people living in close proximity to each other could go as long as you & Peggy without any sexual relations at all. [...] Of course if you deny it – that's that - the only other thing is last year – if you choose to waste your substance on such women as Annie ______ ______ & etc it's your own look out I suppose but you should also remember your responsibilities – your work – James Michael & myself.

I've had two very kind letters from your brother – he is holidaying in the Isle of Mull but coming back next week, but then, you'll have got his note by now – I expect. I think if he wants to come up & see you, you should let him – after all he is your brother & it is nice to be friendly with one another.

I[*'m*] glad you did not see Helen – I had a letter from her, saying she'd stayed the night in Perth & had rung up the Hospital – but as the Matron who knew all about you was out, she did not go up! Ha! Ha!

I meant to write you a long newsy letter but I'm decidedly tired. Have hurled 30 bags of peat home today – my back feels as if its

[63] In the 1930s, i.e. before penicillin, treatment for syphilis involved neoarsphenamine, an organic arsenic compound, by intravenous injection.

permanently bent – neck sore & aching of the skin of the palm of my hands – what a life.

JM & I are managing "no sae bad" – I find I can live on 10/- a week, which is something.

I miss the "mails" these days – only one by the last mail & that from your brother – none from you – Routledges are getting on with *Scottish Eccentrics* – so you need not worry about that.

Now – Christopher dear – is there anything you want? Or would like? Do let me know & if it is possible we'll get it for you – I'm enclosing a few papers – nothing exciting – still they may pass the time a bit for you.

All love - JM sends kisses & hugs

Valda

Isle of Whalsay

13/9/35

My dear Christopher,

I was so glad to get your long letter & to hear you've been so much better this last few days – go on improving laddie.

I saw in the *Radio Times* today that Gordon Bottomley is broadcasting from the (damn this pen nib has broken & JM has lost my own pen)

New Arts Gallery – Perth on Sept. 17th (Tuesday next). – I thought perhaps you could get in touch with him – maybe you'd like to see him if it could be arranged.

I've been working fairly hard since I came back – straightening things out etc etc but have been reading quite a lot of your stuff through again *Sangschaw – Penny Wheep – Northern Numbers – Stony Limits* & I'm ¾ way through *The Drunk Man* – I wish the Glasgow Poem[64] could be up to its standards after reading *The Drunk Man* – all the B.O stuff etc seems not worth doing – trashy –

Re. the paragraph of mine you could not decipher – "It was awfully stupid of you to go to Soutar['*s*][65] – for Heavens sake exercise a little common sense. Dr Chamber[*s*] said it practically undid all the good all the good that had been done" which was perfectly true. After all you were not in a fit condition to walk all the way down into the town for a taxi & then spend 2 – 3 hours talking with Soutar. You know yourself what a rotten weekend you had after it. Don't do that sort of thing again. That's what I've been trying to say. Now that's that old dear.

Like you I'm hoping against hope that the Oban thing[66] comes off – what a difference it would make – give us both a fighting chance.

---

64 'The Red Lion,' started in London in August 1934 (John Manson).

65 William Soutar (1898 – 1943), Perthshire poet. A recent collection, *My Ain Toun* (Brian McCabe, Perth and Kinross Libraries, 2003), contains a photograph of MacDiarmid and Valda at the unveiling of a memorial plaque to Soutar.

66 The Oban Project to launch a paper in Oban which would employ MacDiarmid and bring the family down to Oban from Whalsay - this project was never realised. (John Manson, correspondence).

Nothing came for you today except the *T L Sup* & *The Week* – these I will send on Monday – after Orr has had a look at them.

James Michael is doing fine & is continually asking after you – he saw Lizzie (the Dr's Lizzie)[67] the other day & went over & asked her "Hev you still got my Daddy?"

Do you still get so many headaches? I hope not – I shouldn't bother writing people if I were you, just rest while you have a chance. You'll have to make up for it soon enough.

A very nice letter form Saurat– Yes, I've put it amongst your other stuff.

It has done nothing but rain since I returned. I'll be glad to turn my back on the place – ho! Routledges haven't antied up yet, but Pat is seeing that they do quite soon.

I expect when I've closed this up I'll find I've left unsaid a lot of things & reminds me – I'm sending on to you some *Second Hymns to Lenin* – would you sign them for me & return them immediately. I'm trying to do a little business – what!

Now Chris – dear Christopher

all love

Valda

---

67 Lizzie Williamson. 'She kept house for Dr Orr, whose marriage in May 1933 was very brief, and accompanied him to his new practice in Leith.' – John Manson, in *The New Shetlander* article, ibid.

Isle of Whalsay
Shetland Isles

15/9/35

Orr has just been in –he's on the
prowl for a bottle of whisky – Dirty dog!

Dearest Christopher,

I was awfully pleased to get your letter & to hear that you are improving so rapidly. Don't overdo it, will you? Have they started the treatment yet? Dr Orr is taking a blood test on Friday – it's better to be on the safe side.

By now you will have received my letter & papers. You should, anyway, have got them before this.

Why is F.G. pressing for your discharge – surely it is better to stay on for a week or two longer, for I feel sure once you get out you will not be careful of yourself – you know what a harum-scarum you are.

Will you go to the Scotts for a few weeks? I do not think it would be wise for you to come right back here, much as I would love to have you. As it is I'm living on only a few shillings per week – you must have strengthening food etc etc

Today is Regatta Day – not much life about it. I called in to see Orr this afternoon & he was playing Ludo with Mary Grace (Lizzie's cousin). James Michael was very taken up with the racing. Ran in the boys race 5 years to eight years & completed the course, which I thought was very good for small 'un.

Re. *Red Scotland* – nothing is being done about it – Routledges are not putting it out until January. *Scottish Eccentrics* is OK. The galley proofs have not arrived yet – but will send them on as soon as ever they come. No news, as per usual. It was grand to get the enclosed papers. Did Helen send them to you?

Now, dear one I must away. Will write you again during the weekend. Sorry but I have not money to send you – but you'll understand – I'll enclose a couple of envelopes & some paper the best I can do.

I hear Black has been through to Oban this weekend. We'll soon know the worse.

Goodnight

Yours

Valda

[Misc. part of letter, headed p. 3, MS 27150, folio p. 163.]

3.

You owe him – until you are better – also that he will bring pressure to bear on Mr Warburg to forward the £40 – I told Pat that I wanted it for Dr bills – but you know that I must have it to clear the Whalsay debts – . Pat is going to see *Scottish Eccentrics* through for you & that it is done in the way you want it – I have stressed the fact that you are too ill to write so for goodness sake be still & say 'nuffin' – If there is anything you want to say – about *S.E*'s write me –

Cheerio darling

All my love

Valda

To Somhairle MacGILL-EAIN / Sorley MacLEAN

Isle of Whalsay

15/9/35

Dear MacLean,

I should have written you before – but have been so dreadfully worried - & busy – Christopher collapsed the day after you left & went down to the Dr Orr's — on the following Tuesday night. Orr gave me no hope so I wired F.G. Scott to meet us in Aberdeen & get Christopher down immediately. God! What a journey – I'll never forget it. He is now in a Nursing Home & the Dr.s give him a 30% chance of recovery — they say it's "complete nervous exhaustion" – poor fellow – he's down to just over 8 sts – I did not think he was so emaciated. Did you?

I've been back a fortnight & have been kept busy – soothing irate publishers. Phew!

Last week the news was fairly satisfactory – they had made various test etc & could find nothing organically wrong – also that he'd picked up a bit during the last three or four days – the previous week he'd been very ill but I suppose he will be up & down – one can really expect nothing else – but it is so worrying.

Michael still talks about you - & calls you "my big man". He's still a little devil.

By the way I'm awfully sorry I did not post on the letter that came for you sooner – I hope it contained nothing important – forgive me!

Shall I send the book you sent back to you – or shall I hang on to it for a few weeks until I see what is happening?

Don't you hate being back at school again – after such a long holiday – it must be pretty awful.

My kindest regards
Yours sincerely
Valda Grieve

Will let you know how things go.

Shetland Isles
Sunday Evening
[*22 September 1935*]

My dearest Christopher,

I'm feeling so bucked with Life – after receiving the good news that you are well on the road to recovery – honestly dear – I did not know I loved you so much, until you were so ill – it's just great to be able to feel lighthearted again. Hurry up & get back – I'm impatient for you.

It was nice of Graham to come & see you – he did not lose much time. I thought it was the only right [*sic*] to let him know you were ill. I hope you did not curse me.

I'm enclosing a wedding card addressed to us both. I hadn't the foggiest idea who it can be unless it is Floss MacNeill's[68] sister – but I didn't know she had one. I have not written – perhaps you will.

Orr has received Chambers letter. I think you should write him – he's been awfully decent to you & me – he says he can get the injections for you, free. The Board of Health will supply it & ask no questions.

It is still frightfully cold & miserable – it's been raining every day since I came back.

Michael is still going strong – tonight he cut the leg of his pyjamas. He is still very puzzled at your non-appearance & tells everyone that "he loves you much & that he's got to be a good [*boy*] before you will come back – but bad boy will come out." He[*'s*] getting a bit of queer way of expressing himself. Yesterday evening the sun was shining for a wee while in the back window – you know how the light can rest on objects – that[*'s*] how it was last night. Mikey looked up & saw it & said – "Look Mummy, the sun sitting on the window" which really described it.

[68] Flos (Florence) MacNeill, anthologist, novelist, folklorist, historian, author of *Iona: A History of the Island with Descriptive Notes* (London 1920); *The Scots Kitchen: Its Traditions and Lore, with Old-time Recipes* (London 1929) and other volumes.

I had a letter from Black on Friday – he said he'd had a note from you – nothing yet is definitely fixed up for the Oban thing – Blast it.

The Rev Angus (the man in Mackay's place) is quite nice – he's well on to 70 - & you can't very well dislike him – he's a game old bird. By the way – he knows of you – asked me if you were the same man that used to write for Montrose Standard[69] – has a relative who knew John MacLean – was a great friend of his as matter [*of*] fact. I happen[*ed*] to mention that you were thinking of writing a book on him & the next time I saw him he said he'd written to the man & asked him if he'd any material that would be helpful to you.

Robert was very drunk yesterday when I went up to the shop & told me I was getting "fine paps" on me – much to Magnie's disgust – this is the first time I've heard the expression used (although I knew of it) & it sounds worse than the others - & they are bad enough.

I think Helen sent you *Life & Letters* before she went on holiday – she said there was a belated review of *Scottish Scene* – would you tear it out & keep it. By the way where did you put the photo of your brother & yourself as a baby? I was parcelling up the photo's the other day & could not see it – you might let me know – it's better to have them all together.

Yes! I know about Valentine[70] – before you went there – I'm glad you are staying on a little longer – for goodness sake don't come out too soon. You know, I suppose that Orr has offered to pay "so much" – he's an awfully decent soul. I quite like him now.

Always I find after I've closed any letter to you that I've forgotten a hundred & one things – it is most annoying.

I'm writing to my mother & asking her to send you on a small suitcase (but larger than the one you have) that I left behind last year – you've accumulated a few more things than you went in with. Shall I

69 Christopher lived in Montrose 1921 – 1929 & had worked as chief reporter on the weekly *Montrose Review*.

70 James Valentine (1906 – 2007) was a founder member of the National Party of Scotland, now a doctor in the Gilgal. He also knew Christopher in London c. 1929-30.

send on your black hat – I expect F.G. will need his back again. (You borrowed it to go into the hospital.) I'm enclosing a few hankies – I expect you'll be needing them badly – how are you off for socks? Let me know.

It was good of F.G. to bring you the tob. & pipe[71] I can well imagine how thankful you were to receive them. I'd thought of sending you some tab. but have never managed [*to*] raise it. I'm on an occasional packet of Woodbines these days – I'm not doing so badly. I'm existing on five bobs I got from Orr. So don't worry unduly over me.

Really dear one – I must away – have several more letters to write & I do not feel a bit in the mood for doing them –

Cheerio

All my love

Valda

---

71 'Scott came through on Saturday bringing me black tobacco and a fine new big-bowled pipe. He strongly urged me to stay on here for another month or so....' *NSL*, p. 99.

To William Aitken

Isle of Whalsay
Shetland Isles

24.9.35

Dear Mr Aitken,

Thank you — for your kind letter – Re the Edinburgh Rectorial. I think everything will be all right by then (it's not until the end of Oct., is it?) for I've been getting splendid news of Mr Grieve — during the last ten days or so – he's been making rapid progress & is now allowed up in the forenoons – & will the Dr thinks be strong enough to leave the Nursing Home within a month. Of course he will have to take great care & not over do things for some time – but that will not affect the Rectorial – I do not suppose he will take an active part – like he did at the Aberdeen – I know he wants to – but Edinburgh – I believe is far more to deal with – a stickler for the old conventions.

By now I expect you've heard from Mr Scott.

Yours sincerely

Valda Grieve

Isle of Whalsay
Shetland Isles

27/9/35

My dearest Christopher,

Received your two letters on Wednesday – I'm so looking forward to seeing you again. I can hardly believe it is true. So it is almost sure that the Oban thing is to come off – good – it would be just as well for you to come straight back in that case, as you'll have such a lot of "picking up" of your own stuff to do.

I've found about six red note books, but cannot for the life of me find the poem you want. I know it quite well – have gone through them thoroughly & even dragged the Dr up to a look through them, but I will have another look before I post this. Sorry old dear – you'll have to forgive me.

We haven't had much of a storm, just a couple of days of high wind – but nothing like what you've been having Down South. We've had torrential rain, but that is nothing out of the way here.

No! I have not forgotten the *S. Hymns to Lenin* – I'll send them on now. Could send them on to Helen – she's going to try & get rid of them for me, to help the exchequer so write her a nice little note.

Letters – darling one most unsatisfactory. I'm afraid you've been misunderstanding a lot that I've written to you, possibly my own fault. I'm not awfully good at expressing myself. ~ So we'll say no more about things. ~

I'm glad Scott came down to see you again. It must make a nice change for you.

How did the broadcast of the *Birlinn* go off – did you hear it? I've never mentioned it before because I've been so mad with myself. Your letter came on the Wed. then it was broadcast & somehow or other, it just didn't sink into the old grey matter that it was Wednesday – what a poor [?*coot*] I am. I hope you got paid for it.

I'll send the note along to Pat – but don't you remember Routledges had decided not to publish *Red Scotland* until January in one of their letters to you before you went down to the Dr. I came across the letter after I'd written to Warburg saying "this for political reasons & in view of the forthcoming [?*rectorial*] etc etc etc – You were anxious to have it out this autumn." I had a nice reply from Wisharts, saying if Messrs Routledge still reject it they would be very willing to consider publication etc etc

By the way, how many series of *Contemporary Scottish Studies* are there? Also *Northern Numbers*?

When do you expect to be home? Somewhere round the third week in Oct.. I'm getting quite excited. 'Fraid I haven't done much housework, since I came back – but will do a "spring clean" for your arrival.

Mikey Fike sends love & kisses plus

All mine –

Valda

To Sorley MacLEAN / Somhairle MacGILL-EAIN

POSTCARD

To: S. MacLean Esq.
Elgin Hotel, Portree, Skye
Isle of Whalsay

Dear MacLean,

Thanks for your kind letter. Christopher I'm glad to say has made a remarkably rapid recovery since I last wrote you - & I'm expecting him back tomorrow – it seems too good to be true – the Orrs would rather he stayed in a month or six weeks longer, but you know how obstinate men can be – we hard working females would be only too glad of a few weeks extra rest.

With a struggle I managed to get the proofs of "*Scottish Eccentrics*" & *Stony Limits* poems – corrected & away – a bit late – but still. *Red Scotland* I'm afraid proved too much & it is being held over until January – a pity in view of the fast moving political events - & it would have been nice to have had it out for the Rectorial. I saw R B when in Edinburgh – also had a letter from him last week – he seems very hopeful for the O.P.[72] He was up the weekend before last & saw the crowd there & he's now pretty certain it will come off. I do hope things are [?*brighter*] with you – you have all my sympathy.

Sincerely

Valda Grieve

[72] The Oban Project, as above. My thanks to John Manson for helping me decipher this Postcard.

POST OFFICE TELEGRAPHS

PERTH 2 OCT 35

Office of Origin
WHALSAY

GREAVE GILGAL HOSPITAL PERTH =

DON'T OVERDO THINGS WILL COME HOME = VALDA+

Shetland Isles
Thursday 3rd [*October 1935*]

My dearest Christopher,

I do hope you are taking care of yourself & that you come up cabin, instead of steerage. It is unfortunate that the boats have only changed this week & that'll [*mean*] you have to be up on early Monday morning. I will try & get Duddy to fetch you in the car – do be a sweet soul & take a "first" class ticket, the "*Earl*." By the way, do try & see if there are any Whalsay boats going up on Sat. night – I know one or two are down there.

It is awfully late gone 2 a.m. – I'm deadly tired, have been doing a bit of spring cleaning for your benefit – old dear – say Thank you very much! Orr has a bad cold, no wonder the weather we've been having.

If you have some money & some time, will you go to Lipton's & get me the following. I really need them

3 lbs dried Fruit Salad @ 6D lb.
2 lbs prunes @ 6D per lb
1 lbs streaky bacon for frying

&

if you are in funds, you can get some peas & tinned fruit. But these aren't necessary.

Looking forward so much to seeing you darling

all my love

Valda

Poor Mikey Fike is trying to learn a piece of poetry to say to you – you're coming so soon – is rather hurrying the process. I said you'd give him 2 pennies if he said it.

Another separation occurred in the summer of 1936. The whole family appear to have been away from Whalsay – then Valda and James Michael travelled to Cornwall, presumably because of the illness of Valda's Mother and Aunt, although in October 1935 Christopher had wanted Valda to take James Michael to Cornwall anyway 'and leave him there for a month or so'[73] *whilst he established a place for the family in Oban.*

Christopher travelled back to Whalsay the same day, Monday 18th May, and having arrived to find the cottage locked and being unable to gain entry, lodged with Dr Orr for a week or so. Although still receiving treatment, he reports he's in fine fettle and is indeed back working at his earlier intensity on an astonishing number of projects. In addition to journalism and poetry these include his autobiography, the official biography/memoir of the writer and politician Cunninghame Graham[74]*, a book* Speaking for Scotland *and preparations for several upcoming broadcasts, not to mention the voluminous correspondence.*

James Michael is now 3 years and 9 months old.

---

[73] see *NSL*, p. 104.

[74] The National Trust for Scotland maintains a memorial cairn to Cunninghame Graham at Gartmore.

28 King Street
Bude
Monday Evening
[*May 1936*]

Christopher dear,

Received your most welcomed letter this morning & it is a relief to know that you have recovered from the harassing Friday morning – it sounds too good to be true. The journey down was I suppose no sae bad – of course JM was on the "go" the whole time but fortunately he was not fretful. Rather a nuisance but we had to change at Exeter – the lights failed in our coach, then we had the usual change at Okehampton & to top all – the gas gone out & we had to change again at Halwill. We finally arrived here at 9.30 pm. What a life!

Things here are pretty bad – my aunt is really very ill. She's been in bed for five weeks suffering from pernicious anemia (can't spell it) & it is affecting her heart – she is wanting to go to the Exeter hospital for 2 months. Other two are on the verge of a breakdown & on the border of lunacy.

JM came out with an extraordinary remark the night he arrived – all he would say was "Daddy away away" (& he's been saying it ever since) so my aunt trying to comfort him happened to say "Where is daddy?" "Daddy away, away in museum sitting down." Naturally I could scarcely believe it but on putting him to bed I was saying the usual goodnight he repeated it – probably it was due to his brain being over tired for he has not said it again – rather strange wasn't it?

About the 26th I'm in a fever of excitement & anxiety – I trust to God you'll carry it through alright. May the blessing of the little people & the luck of the Devil be with you & yours.

I'm sorry you're having legal trouble with Gollancz – libel I suppose ye hot-headed deil. I sincerely hope it will not delay publication.[75]

[75] Gollancz had published *Stony Limits and Other Poems* (London, 1934). Fear of legal action led to several alterations in the first edition, but the original poems were later restored in *Stony Limits and Scots Unbound* (Edinburgh: Castle Wynd Printers Limited, 1956).

How is Nancy K. in full bloom? - & the rest of the gang? Helen I presume you've managed to dodge.

How is the "dough" holding out? Better than mine I trust. Before I could take JM out they made me buy him a new coat. I fell as well for a beige coat, red frock & hat – the total for this being £3.15.6 (not too bad – far less expensive than [?]) Stockings & pyjamas sort of [?] extras – now I'm fairly decent to look at - "but my face is my fortune Sir" she said – but do not let that worry you.

Down here it's been very hot (the weather I mean) far too warm for this time of the year. Christopher I'd never realised how wonderful – soul inspiring it is to be awakened by the singing of the birds. Laugh I don't care.

Thule[76] is enjoying much admiration from the males – they flock around her like bees – what my aunt says is of course another story.

My box etc have not arrived

[*letter ends here – pages missing*]

[76] James Michael's dog – JM took Thule back to Shetland, where they became very attached, to the extent of JM writing to his father prior to he and his mother moving to Glasgow to join Christopher that he would have to stay in Shetland for a very long time should he not be able to take Thule with him.

28, King Street
Bude
Nth Cornwall

20/5/36

Dearest Christopher,

I've [?] just a few things – only arrived home last night after a tiring journey – took JM into the Hospital – God they made my blood boil. They treat one just like cattle. His name has been put on the vacancy list. I suppose if I'd been prepared, I could have got it done for nothing, but when the blasted woman asked me in such a contemptuous voice if I could afford to pay £3 for the operation,[77] I said 'Yes.'

I'm enclosing a few Penguin books – hang on to them as I've nearly all the first series. Now don't forget to send one of the parcels & roll up your dirty washing & send on.

By the way, in the clothes cupboard, left-hand side facing the cupboard, about 3rd or fourth shelf down a[*re*] white wool knitted knickers – unfinished – you could send them on with your clothes. Expect the place is horribly damp. I do wish you'd go down to the Dr.

I hear the articles you've fixed up are to be about Langholm – sounds good – do write & tell me all news.

I'm longing to be with you again – I grudge all the days we are not together.

Give my apologies to Mrs Bruce etc for not writing - & will now that things are going on alright.

All my love darling

Valda

---

[77] Ear Nose & Throat operation - tonsillectomy.

28, King Street
Bude

14/6/36
10.30pm

My Darling Christopher,

I'm so sorry to have kept you so long without a letter – but I've been kept so busy. I hardly know which way to turn.

I fetched JM on Wednesday – poor little soul, it has taken it out of him. He's just a ghost of his former self. I hope he'll pick up soon, because I want to get back to you as quickly as possible.

Are you taking care of yourself? How are you off for money? Let me know if you want any – I would have sent you some more today, only I've only one cheque left. Perhaps you could drop the bank a note to send me another book. Have the Langholm articles appeared yet – I heard you were doing them.

I received the snaps from Mrs Bruce – thought they were awfully good, also letter from Auntie Betty, which I will answer next week – honestly old dear you may not believe it, but I haven't been as far as the breakwater – never seem to get a minute to spare in the evening. Well I'm too darned tired to want to go out – had rather a rough passage last week – must have been the medicine I'm taking I think – was in agonies of pain in my tummy for three days. You can guess I was pretty bad, for Aunt Jane had to give me brandy – whew! Hope it doesn't occur again.

Was rather amused to hear of the Dr's flitting – as Auntie B. remarked, "it's the limit."

By the way, you know the yellow jumper I enclosed in the parcel – when Mrs Mainland returns it you need not send it on to me again – I'll not be needing it.

Mother is getting on slowly – she's rather depressed these days – feels sure she'll never see me again, poor little soul, she probably won't either. I – oh! What's the use of meeting trouble half way.

We're still having dreadful weather – last Friday was good, but I had to take advantage of it & washed with Aunt Jane's help six big blankets & our divan cover. Saturday & today it's been raining hard – nice sort of rain though – refreshing.

I've done up three parcels of laundry & will start sending them back. I wouldn't open them if I were you – but put them somewhere dry, until I come back. I'll start back the first week in July – mother wants me to have my birthday at home, otherwise I would come back the week before. What shall I do about registering JM – think perhaps I should try & work it in, altho' it will be awkward with JM – but perhaps I could leave him with Willie Johnstone family for a day – will you write him – or shall I? I do not have his address with me. He has to be registered at Storrington – you remember the place – about 3 miles from Thakeham.

Expect I'll get a letter from you tomorrow morning – I do look forward to your letters so much & I'm missing you all the time, for I do love you such a lot, my darling.

JM thinks it time to be going to[*o*] – several times this week he's asked "When are we going back to Scotland & Daddy.["] The nurses told me he was asking for you, more than he was me, when in the hospital. You know I was bit nervous lest he should make a song about the smacking you gave him – they were asking him one day – "if Daddy was good to him" – I was "listening in" at the foot of the stairs – "Daddy never smacks me at all – but Mummy smacks me all the time" – little blighter.

How are the injections serving you – not having any bad effects I hope – on mouth.

What are you working on now? Have you finished the University book yet - & how is the *Cornish Song* getting on – are you still working on it? What happened about Dents – did Church take the Mature Art?

'Fraid I'll have to stop, now – must try & write Mrs Bruce[78] tomorrow night – I'm nearly asleep –

[78] May have been matron or a nurse in the Gilgal. She had written to Christopher asking Valda to knit her a jumper – John Manson.

Good night, my darling
All my love
Valda

Received parcels – snaps etc – if there is another parcel – that looks as if it might be laundry – still there – send it on per return, will you, so that I can get it washed up quickly.

V.

Monday

Received letter & book etc this morning – just received second one by midday post. Worried to hear you're not sleeping – still my dear one – only 3 more weeks & I'll be with you.

No I haven't heard anything from Nurse Bruce or Neil Gunn- . Looking forward to reading typescript of your *Autobio.*[79] Have you done more to the *Cornish Song*[80]? Do for goodness sake take care of yourself - & get out as much as you can – for grub & other things – 5 mins to catch post All love. Valda.

PS

What happened to the typewriter? Did you get it seen to – or not?

79 Christopher dedicated his autobiography *Lucky Poet* 'to my wife Valda Trevlyn Grieve'.

80 Poem '*Cornish Heroic Song for Valda Trevlyn*' (1939).

28, King Street
Bude
Nth Cornwall

21/6/36

My dearest Christopher,

Have just had a lovely warm tub & a hair wash – outside it is raining heavily - plus thunder & lightning – would love to be out on the cliffs now.

Thanks awfully for the cigarette case & contents. The latter came just at the right time - & I do like the case – very much.

Only another fortnight darling & that will soon slip – I hate you being up there all alone. I hope you really don't think I'm paying you back in your own coin re. letters – I'm not – never even crossed my mind – I know I've been frightfully remiss, but honestly I can't help it. The condition[*s*] here are really hard & they're all too vague to put down on paper.

I'm feeling quite a bit better – still have the attacks of giddiness occasionally, but looking very much better.

How is the Dr getting on? & what is happening re. the house – are the authorities taking steps to remedy the matter or is he getting marching orders?

I'm glad to hear you're going out a bit visiting various people – it'll do you the world of good.

Nearly all my laundry etc is packed up – yesterday I washed your old grey coat & pressed it – the latter job was done 1.50 a.m. this morning – mums the word.

The air mail, then, makes no difference – I thought if I posted a letter Monday you'd be sure to get it on Wed. or Thursday the latest - & yet you say "Friday – the earliest" – what a blow!

Tomorrow I'm going to the dentist to have three teeth out & I'm funking it – I'm sure to make an ass of myself – on this pathetic note – I'll away –

Cheerio my own darling

there isn't long to wait now –

All my love

Valda

PS

Don't forget to write & ask the bank to send me another cheque book – otherwise I'll not be able to get back.

By the way – did you receive patterns of ribbon from B[?] – a brocade – if there is one the colour & width – order a yard & ask them to forwarded [*sic*] it on to me – that will save time.

Will leave this open until tomorrow – there is sure to be a letter from you in the morning.

Monday

Meant to have add a bit more this morning – but I've been to the dentist & had one of my back teeth out – it was a brute – 3 great roots & each root going in a different direction

[*separate page – torn*]

The dentist said – he has not pulled out such a difficult tooth in a female for a long time. It was a good job I'd forgotten that I had the fellow one out in London when in business & the dentist there had to stop three times & draw breath - & rest or something before he got it out.

God! My face – ears & teeth are all aching like hell – hope they'll soon stop – laugh! I nearly kicked the dentist a good one in the tummy – just missed – which was lucky for us both. To be [?] .

28, King Street
Bude
Thursday morning
[*25 June 1936*]

My darling,

Received your four letters & book this morning – darling I'm terribly sorry I've caused you any unnecessary worry – I know I've not been a model wife, but honestly Christopher – you're scarcely ever out of my thoughts – I mean it.

My reason for not writing – I thought I'd told you – I'm up at 6 – 6.30 a.m. every morning & I'm on until 10pm sometimes later - & as you can guess by then that I'm all in – my nerves are in a shocking condition – I feel sure that more than half my trouble is being away from you.

Worried – I'm worried to death over you but I don't see how I can get back any sooner – I went on Monday to the dentist on Monday [*sic*] & had one extraction – it was very difficult & altho' the place is healing up beautifully I've been in a terribly lot – pain. Went down this morning to have another out – but he won't do it until Monday – this time he's given me some pills to take the night before. Sort of nerve soother, I suppose.

I have two more to come out & about 3 to be filled – the filling won't take long & I'll start as soon as he has finished – I've packed all my parcels & I'm now in the midst of packing my blue case.

That leaves only my personal case to pack. So it really sounds as if I'm nearly on the way. Suppose I really ought to go down to Storrington – think I'll write to the Johnstone's & ask if they'll put me up for a night – they can look after JM while I pop down. I can then get the night bus to Edinburgh. Stay one night there & catch the boat at Aberdeen – once I get underway I'll not stay a minute more than I can help anywhere.

Thanks for books – up to now I haven't had time to read any of them – I have partly read *The Body's Rapture*[81], but was so interrupted in the last section – *Lord God*[82] – that I did not refer to it in my letter – as I wanted to reread it.

I'm glad Davey[83] is coming up – it will help the time to pass - & act as a [?].

Re photo – if I can I'll get it done – that is if my face improves a bit first now I look quite forty – plus a swollen face, puffy eyes – for goodness sake, darling be diplomatic - - the frank & fearless style is all very well – if it is kept within limits otherwise it is apted [*sic*] to be misunderstood.

Gosh! There should be some fun in Oct. – I hope this time it will be properly organised.

I sent a wire to you today – because I doubt that you'll get this letter until Wednesday next – my letters seem to take so very much longer than yours.

Betty has a baby girl – had word this morning – weighed 9 lbs. Both doing well.

Will write you again this weekend without fail – give Harriet my love & do explain to her the reason for my not writing.

All my love
Darling
Valda

81 Christopher had sent *The Body's Rapture* by Jules Romains (a translation from the French by John Rodker had been published in London in 1933) and H.J. Muller's *Out of the Night: A Biologist's View of the Future* with his letter of 20 June 1936, saying, 'I would like you to read it carefully and get all its information and ideas thoroughly into your head – as I am increasingly interested in all these vital matters and anxious to have you able to discuss them with me if you too are interested, as I hope you will be.' (*NSL*, p. 125).

82 The book is in fact in three sections: 1. *Lucienne* 2. *The Lord God of the Flesh* and 3. *When the Ship* … . The *Lord God* section includes descriptions of the intensity of the first sexual experiences of a newly married couple; the book is a literary manifestation of the eroticism appearing in the work of French visual artists at the time (Surrealists).

83 George Elder Davie (1912 – 2007) a philosopher who has written extensively on the Scottish Enlightenment as well as other subjects, e.g. a pamphlet 'The Social Significance of the Scottish Philosophy of Common Sense' records a lecture he gave at the University of Dundee in 1972.

Haven't time to reread this – Aunt Jane's calling – I believe she has sadistic tendencies.
PTO There's no fear Christopher dear of my ever stopping loving you – you're my whole world – I love you so much

In bed
1.45 a.m.
[*28 June 1936*]

Darlingest,

Do you see it is getting late – have been frightfully busy all the evening – written 15 letters – Phew! Have written to the Registrar etc to fix up a date.[84] Now that he has written again I may as well get it over, it only means staying a night in London & I can make that up, by catching the first boat once I get to Scotland. Also wrote William Johnstone asking him if I could leave JM with them for a day.

I was so glad I got all your letters together, the last time, or I should have been so much more worried else – darling you must never doubt my love for you. I do love you – in every way a woman should love her husband. Although we've had some hard times together, I've never regretted it – as you know – the only time I've really felt bitter toward you was that time at Longniddry, but that is over now. In any case, even then, if anything had happened to part us, I'd have been more unhappy away from you than with you – so that's that. Life is anything but dull with you, & I am intensely interested in all you do & I haven't money or much time as I would like to have to read & study.

It is unfortunate in many ways that every thing is so crude in our cottage, no convenience at all – plus the extra amount of time it takes to do anything to the water etc etc, but still it has its compensations my dear.

Barely a fortnight now & we'll be together again – I just dare not say anything.

I'm so glad Davie will be with you this week. How long is he staying? Hope it a week or longer – it will take you out of yourself.

Will try & get a saffron cake for you tomorrow. It's so hot just now – otherwise I would have sent you some pasties & butter but they would never keep this weather.

---

84 Registering James Michael at Storrington, as mentioned in previous letter.

Have had JM in bed this weekend with a strained tummy nothing serious, but it's been rather painful. He & I are in the house alone to-night (confess I feel a bit frightened). Mother has gone up to Poughill for a week – she gets out of bed for a couple of hours each day & the Doc said she could go, if she went by car (not bus) & went very slowly. Aunt Jane walked up this afternoon & evidently she's staying the night as it's 2 o'clock & no sign of her. Had a fine spate of letter writing this evening – can't write or do anything when she's about – nerves, I suppose.

Hope there will be a nice long letter from you tomorrow – Blast n hell – have to go to the dentist tomorrow & have another tooth out. God only knows what I'll do if my nerves ache like they did with the last one. This is the only day I've been practically free from pain & I had it out last Monday.

Have lost 9 lbs. since I came home – it doesn't notice. So cheerio.

Will write a bit to this tomorrow, if I hear from you.

Just going to take the pill the dentist gave me – can't see what good it's going to do – here's hoping –

Goodnight, my own darling
All my love
Valda

Monday morning
[29 *June 1936*]

No luck this morning, no letter from you – couldn't get a saffron cake at the shop & the dentist wouldn't draw another tooth- the one hasn't healed up properly & here I am half doped. The pills have made me so sleepy & comfortable – have to go down on Wednesday. That's my birthday rotten luck isn't it – sorry to forget in my last letter to tell you when it was – never mind – I'll let you know all about that when I see you. I was wondering, if it's not possible for me to get my photo done while down here – can't have it done with a swollen face – then perhaps I could have it done in Edinburgh – in time for publication. Perhaps I could come down with you for the Rectorial[85] – let me know what you think. I'll try & get it done but don't be disappointed if I don't.

Perhaps there will be a letter from you by the midday post. I hope so.

Cheerio my darling,

I'll be glad when we're together again –

All my love

Valda

[85] Edinburgh University Rectorial Election.

Tuesday night

30/6/36

My dearest Christopher,

This is just a short note – to catch the Thursday boat – not much news – have nearly finished packing – just a few odds & ends left now.

Went up to the Dr last night – had a blood test – my blood was up several points – he said carry on with the pills & tonic for another month & then get the Doc to give you a test & if you're up – can leave it off.

Also said my nerves were in a very bad state (which is true) & that what I needed was "a jolly good holiday & to get back to your husband as quickly as you can" – oh yeah! – Dr's orders darling – so look out.

I'm going down to the dentist tomorrow to have the other tooth out & I'm in a blue funk. Perhaps I'll be OK once I get down there – but just now I'm feeling dreadful – silly ass.

No letter from yesterday to today – but I expect Davie is with you.

Heavy rain & thunder here today – I quite enjoyed it.

JM is doing fine – went to Poughill in the bus all by himself – felt very proud of himself.

Cheerio for now my darling we'll soon be with you –

All love

Valda

Wednesday

[*1 July 1936*]

Feeling rather better now – the dentist wouldn't pull out my tooth – I'd worked myself up into such a state – so have to go down tomorrow. Isn't it bloody – of course I should have gas & be done with it – only I can't bear the thoughts of going & - only a few days left before I start – hey oh – will be glad when I see you again –

All love

Valda

30 today - Gawd blimey!

28, King Street
Bude
8/7/36

Darling!

This is just a short scribble – want to get it off before tea. Received your wire today – so glad there is direct boat earlier than Tuesday – this means I'll be home on Tuesday – won't it? For goodness sake don't go getting yourself in gaol before I get back – I can't bear to be away from you much longer. I'm going to Glasgow for the week-end – Sat. & Sunday - & will get down to Edinburgh & catch the boat at Aberdeen.

All news when we meet – forgot to say I'm going down to Storrington on Thursday to register JM. Hope I'll be lucky & not meet anyone – also that I'll be staying with Chubby in Glasgow.

Mrs J. Tennett
41, Dudley Drive
Hyndland
Glasgow

If I have time will call in to see the Scotts –

All love to you dear one.   Valda

A briefer separation in December 1936, with Christopher in Edinburgh, having finished several books including Red Scotland. *In addition to the reading material mentioned here, Christopher also 'now had a source of good literature and journalism; his friend Bill Aitken, working in the Scottish Central Library, sent him newspaper cuttings and parcels of books – modern novels as well as philosophical works.'*[86]

A particularly difficult letter to decipher – for a new reason, which Valda comes to.

Whalsay Isle
Sunday

Dearest Christopher,

I feel awfully guilty – over the hellish scrawl I sent you – but I have missed you - & will be awfully glad when you get back. Empire day is doing you a good turn after all – for you will be able to come up in the *Earl* (starting from Lerwick 9 a.m.) instead of going over to Isbister & catching the [?]

A few pamphlets of Pro.B.F.s [*Barker Fairley's*] have arrived from Dents – also a book on Goethe.

We've had the first terrible weather – fierce winds – blowing a gale thunder & lightning hail – etc etc – today it has been a little better. The Doc has neglected me – he called once but I was out. I hear he has been living at the Manse – why this [?] ? Never thought he was so keen on them – damn I'll have to stop & light the lamp – can hardly see. That reminds me how are things with your eyes? How do you look in goggles? Big Bad Wolf – eh!

---

[86] Brian Smith in *MacDiarmid in Shetland*, from his interview with Bill Aitken, Dunblane, 11 Aug. 1991.

If you should have any spare pennies – you could go to Liptons & get me –

2 lb. Currants
2 lbs sultanas
2 tins Baked Beans
2 Packets of cereal
Farex or Shredded Wheat etc

This won't come to 5/.

JM & I will be down to the Pier – if fine – with the proper amount of [?] & bunting & the correct amount of gladness on our [?] etc. It's nearly 11.30 pm & I still have a chair to paint - So will away

All my love

Valda

In September 1937 Christopher visited Sorley MacLean & family on Raasay; he also visited Eigg, Skye, South Uist, Barra, Mull and Iona for his book The Islands of Scotland which appeared in June 1939.

To William Aitken

[Acc. 10488/1, folio p. 3]
[Hugh MacDiarmid headed notepaper]

WHALSAY,
VIA LERWICK,
SHETLAND ISLANDS

Sept. 12th

Hello Angelface !

Dear Bill,

Christopher is away just now hiking around Arisaig with a friend, MacCall, Do you know him? I'm sorry but he has taken "Six thousand years of Gaelic grandeur" with him — I have sent him a card asking him to post it back to you – but I'm doubtful whether it will reach him before he starts back – he's expected to be back on Friday next — Do hope the delay will not cause a bother for you.

Here, we have been storm bound for nearly a week. On Friday the *Earl* failed to put in an appearance with the mail — so you can guess what it's been like — Today however has been lovely — rather too good I'm afraid — Did you have good weather for your holiday at Anstruther?

The news re George is cheering & it is quite a relief to know he is not going to Germany — no wonder Mrs Davie had the wind up — The Profs. certainly have plenty of imagination whatever else they lack —[87]

I was going to enclose some snaps but on looking them out - find that already they are fading — will have to send them back as they were only printed last month. When you write again will you send the neg. of CM - M and myself on the beach - Your snaps have come out much better than mine —

Forgive this scrawl - but it's after 1 AM — dreadfully sleepy

Sincerely

Valda

PS

Certainly - I would love a letter all to myself - power to your elbow.

[87] John Manson (correspondence): 'George Elder Davie had been advised to study in Germany - later changed to France - in order to make a complete break from his involvement with MacDiarmid, i.e. supporting his causes instead of studying philosophy.'

The Mystery at Kensington Square
The Murder Caroline Bundy
Rymon Mystery
The Man who killed Fortescue
The Scarlet Messenger
The Murders in Praed Street [88]

17/9/37
12.30pm

Dear Christopher,

Many thanks for postcards & wires – if I realised you were staying longer I would have sent these on before. I hope it is not too late & that you will get them before you leave Lochboisdale.

I am glad you are having a good & interesting time – this holiday should really do you the world of good & there will be really be no excuse when you come back to say you're on the brink of a nervous breakdown.

I've enclosed letter which came from [?*Donald*] today with a couple of books – I am very surprised & annoyed to know that you have been borrowing money from him – surely £19.15 was enough to last you a fortnight in Edinburgh. I'm tired & fed-up with unexpected bills coming in. Surely you have some control over yourself. If it is not too much to ask you – I would be grateful if on the homeward voyage you would spend as little as possible – after posting this – I will have 7 ½ left – it is the regatta tomorrow & I'm afraid Michael will have to go without the usual 6p he expects & should have – I'm afraid now I have little patience with your concern for Christine & Walter – at least they are well clothed & have the things that make a child's life worth living. [89] Michael was wet through several times last week – his mac. is too short & tight & his rubber boots leak water.

[88] Should you visit Brownsbank, instead of the book on Goethe, etc. or at least piles of *Times Literary Supplements*, you will find the bookshelves in MacDiarmid's room full of these sort of murder mysteries. Valda's D.H. Lawrence novels are still in her room.

[89] Christopher's alimony payments were £100 per annum for each child and expenses (*NSL*, p. 118), but he could never afford to pay.

After the Gilgal business you led me to expect a straight deal & it is evident you're not man enough to keep your word or control yourself. Because you have brains you think, I believe, that you can do anything - & expect everything from me — . Expect on, Laddie.

As Gay Taylor says Even a worm will turn - Cheerio

Valda

the 'tec books are in at Symbister – have got the enclosed.

Sunday

Evening. 12.15 pm

[1938]

My dear Christopher,

I was very glad to get your wire – for I was wondering if you managed to get through all right. Do trust you had a decent journey, not too rough and stormy. We've had dreadful weather – not rough – but so very wet.

Both JM & I are down with beastly colds again – this must be the fifth I've had since July, I think – getting a bit too thick. Don't you think?

How are you feeling – very much better I hope. The change of food etc should do you the world of good, that is if you do not over do it in other ways.

Things are going on here much the same as usual – today being Sunday we had breakfast at 11.30 a.m. – and dinner at 4.45 pm – tea & supper all in one, but we made up for it in between, by giving the back kitchen a clean up, which it was badly needing.

How do you find the Scotts? Give Mrs Scott & F.G. my very kindest regards, also Lovey & Frances & the boys. Tell Lovey I thought she was going to write me.

There was nothing for you in the Thursdays mail, except Barker Fairleys letter, my Reader's Union book came. Huxley's "*Ends and Means.*" I'm wondering what tomorrow will bring forth. My mother has gone into hospital – my aunts were not able to [?] the job of looking after her. They are both pretty low down I gather from their letters – poor souls.

On Thursday night I went over to the nurse's – Dr Hulse[90] & Agnes Spence came as well – we went over in the Dr's car, which was very nice, as it was a beastly night.

90 Locum after Dr Orr's departure from Whalsay.

Dr Hulse came up on Wednesday afternoon to ask you to go down to Auntie Betty's for a game – she was very surprised to find you had gone & more than disgusted to learn you'd gone with "that stuff on your face." I heartily agreed with her. Perhaps it's off by now?

By the way why don't you call into the photographer. I forget the name – but you'll remember, the one who wrote you, asking if he could take your photograph the next time you were down. They were at Glasgow Fair, if I remember rightly.

It is getting late & I'm very sleepy (as usual) – will leave this open in case anything turns up tomorrow.

Goodnight my dear

my Love

Valda

PS
I'm forwarding letters – a bundle of papers came today from Helen. I hope you've written Harraps a discreet letter – it seems a great pity that they feel as they do about the Doctors books[91] – they were so keen at the start – after all – if other things like the *Voice of Scotland* etc are going to divert you from putting time in on the things that our very scanty supply of bread & butter comes from – then I doubt if its worth it, for altho' I know its an organ that is needed & that it's good – in the last analysis I doubt if it'll do much to rouse its readers & after all are they worth it – it's [*sentence continues around the edge of page & in space by signature:*] your own stuff you should be doing & trying to get the wherewithal to carry on & do it. I must ask you to be careful & not incur any more debts while down. As Helen says our balance is pitifully small & we've nothing to look forward to. You won't like this, I know but I'm worried I seem to be snowed under just now with Bills & no hope to settle them.

---

91 '*A Pageant of Scottish Doctors*' which was never published.

Another trip away for Christopher at the end of November 1938, to Glasgow to attend a PEN[92] function 3rd December, a dinner in honour of William Power, journalist and author.

Sodom

Wednesday morning

[*end Nov./beg. December 1938*]

My dearest Christopher,

I meant to have written you last night – but I fell asleep as usual - & only awaken about 12 o'clock (Grant was out getting his hair cut) & then had to have a bath. So I got up half an hour earlier this morning to write this – heroic of me. What!

Darling, I was so glad to get your letter this morning – but sorry to hear you're not staying at the Scotts – but perhaps you'll be able to have a few days there next week – I hope you will because it will give you a chance of a rest & someone to talk to.

What a ghastly journey – heaven forbid – I should ever travel that way. I'm glad you had somewhere to wait when in Scalloway.

We've finished all the cleaning here now. I've bathed & washed my hair – Grant's doing his today – tonight he is going over to the Smith's for bridge. I'll have an early night – I think – I hope.

I've made some jolly good draught bags for the back door & outer door – they do make a difference.

Your jacket arrived from the cleaners – like new – I'm putting a patch on the elbows of the same material – cut from waistcoat & it will do you for Bridge nights for long enough.

---

[92] The acronym stands for 'Poets Essayists & Novelists' although this international organisation of writers campaigning for freedom of expression includes writers of all forms. MacDiarmid helped to found the Scottish Centre of International PEN as distinct from the English branch, and the Scottish Centre remains so to this day.

I'm sending on a few letters that came today. Dugald sent a few papers – but they[*'ll*] wait until you come home. I'm writing him by Fridays mail.

I'm dreadfully sorry my last letter ended so – "so-so" but I was frightfully worried - & didn't want to spoil your holiday – but I think perhaps it would have been better had I told you. Hays & Co. account is closed for everything – I went down to order coal – Mr Williams was very nice indeed about it – but said he couldn't possibly let us open a new account until the other one had been paid off – or most of it at any rate. He goes to Lerwick with the books in February & he hopes something will be paid before then – as he said it's a big account for them & Mr Garrick the manager will only give him a blowing up for allowing it to get so big – last year he had a row for allowing an account to reach £30 without payment before February. He has let me have a couple of bags of coal to last until you come home – but I'm to pay him (when I can) – he's not putting in the books..

I must admit he really was very decent – so it's no use getting het up about it. I expect we'll manage somehow.

If you want a £1 – write & let me know – I expect I'll be getting the £5 from Helen tomorrow.

Couldn't you try & get some articles in the *Bulletin* – under a pseudonym – that would keep us going until the books are finished.

Mr & Mrs Power have sent JM a lovely Hornby train & a huge box of paints (the paints I'm keeping over for X'mas, he hasn't seen them) but he's delighted with the train & is now determined to save up to buy bridges & tunnels etc etc. have a good [“*blow*” ??-*illeg.*] time, dear Christopher – for it’s not much you[*’re*] coming back to.

All my love

Valda

PTO
PS

Grant just up – sends his best wishes & hopes you are enjoying yourself more than somewhat.

Sunday night

[1938]

My dearest Christopher,

I'm wondering how you got on yesterday – I thought of you quite a lot and trust everything went off with a swing – how did you come through the two "do's"[93]— I hope the first one didn't lay you out.

It's pouring with rain & has done so continually for the last 6 hours. Damn it!

I forgot to mention in my previous letters that the MSS etc has been sent off to Norman MacLeod.[94]

Haven't cleared cheque from Helen yet – so cannot send you anything. I'm worried – wondering how you are managing for tobacco and things.

Things are going on here just the same – tomorrow night I'm having my "making"[95] and on Tuesday I thought I'd have the nurse up.

Had my tea in bed this morning – Grant got up & made tea put the fire in & went back to bed again. I meant to get some early nights while you were away, but we've been keeping dreadful hours, and I don't see any hope this week of them being any better.

How is F.G. hope he is better & that you'll be able to spend a few days with him. How was Helen looking? I'm longing to hear all about it.

Mr Bruce[96] is very ill, in Lerwick – he couldn't finish his rent collecting. I hear two Drs have been called in – how far that is true I don't know. Dr Hulse has been in Lerwick for the week-end. I'll hear from her tomorrow how things really are. Mrs Bruce sent for Joan to come to Lerwick to help – I presume they are staying at Mrs Hays.

93 The PEN event and possibly his appointment with the Scottish Secretariat of the Communist Party which had been arranged for 6th or 7th December and which he failed to attend.

94 American poet (1906 – 1985).

95 Valda's anglicised version of Shetland dialect *makkin* – or knitting evening.

96 Mr W.A. Bruce, Laird of Whalsay.

A crossword I did the week the papers didn't come until Monday was right, but of course I hadn't sent it away – a lot of readers got it correct that week, but they received £48 odd each. That would have done us all right, wouldn't it. I'm sending one away on Monday, but I expect my chances of winning are passed – I've been so near these last few weeks.

Will keep this opened in case I hear from you tomorrow morning.

By the way if you have managed to scrounge some dough from somewhere you could bring home a 1/- tube of Glycerine Jelly for my hands also a tube Regesan Winter Balm from Boots chemist and three or four coat hangers with bars on them.

Have an awful lot of letters to write but doubt if I'll get many done – feeling dreadfully sleepy.

All my love

Valda

PS
In case you see Orr. I hear his wife is teaching at Burravoe.

Monday

No letter this morning.

Helen's cheque arrived – but haven't had time to change it. Hope you won't need any – but let me know if you do.

"Sodom"[97]

Dear Christopher,

I'm forwarding to you a few letters – please note one from Batsfords[98] goodness only knows what excuse you will try & fob them off with next.

One of my letters returned from the Central Hotel. I should have thought you would have left your address.

We went to the wedding on Thursday last – had a very good time indeed. I got to bed 6.40 a.m. Grant – later. I won't bore you with a description of it.

Trust you are having a good time at F.G's Perhaps you would let me know when to expect you back & I could then meet the boat.

Grant sends his regards.

Yours

Valda

PS

I've written Batsfords saying practically the same thing as I said to Gilbert & Wright – "had bout 'flu – order away for a change." Had a long letter from Barbara today.

---

97 Valda's quotation marks perhaps acknowledge her anglicised spelling of *Sudheim*. By 1942 she was using Sudheim

98 Publisher, waiting for *The Islands of Scotland* manuscript.

Part 2

The War Years

After the War started the trips away from the island were no longer possible. Money was so tight that Valda, Michael and the young man who had come to Whalsay to act as Christopher's secretary-typist, Grant Taylor, stepped up their efforts to collect seabirds' eggs and also collected driftwood on the seashore. Christopher tried to learn how to cut peats, without a great deal of success. Up until 1941, they'd had £1 a week – even this more or less disappeared.[99]

On 23rd December 1941 Christopher had written to his brother, "the meshes of National Service are closing over me as I write."[100] *Deemed unfit for active service, MacDiarmid was conscripted to Glasgow to work in a munitions factory. It is said that had it not been for Helen Cruickshank's intervention, he would have been sent to work on the roads. He left Whalsay on 4th February 1942, while Valda and Michael remained.*

The Grieves had been vehemently opposed to the conscription of Scots – and Cornishmen – in the Second World War and 'even after he accepted industrial conscription MacDiarmid's views do not appear to have altered. At a meeting in Glasgow in April 1942, he declared, "The Scots people had better be careful lest, while they were being beguiled into taking a leading part in fighting for Imperialism, with the thought that they were fighting against Fascism, they found themselves in the grip of Fascism at home." '[101]

99 Brian Smith's essay in *MacDiarmid in Shetland.*

100 *NSL* pp. 199-200.

101 John Manson's article in *The New Shetlander.* The quote from the meeting was recorded in a report by the Glasgow Chief Constable submitted to the Scottish Home Department.

Sudheim
Whalsay
Monday 9th Feb. [*1942*]

My dearest Christopher,

Thank God for the wire – I was dreadfully worried – wondering what on earth had happened to you. Wednesday till Monday seemed a devil of a time. What an awful journey you must have had – I hope you had enough money to see you through – longing to hear all news. This is only a short scrawl – have had a hectic time today. G & I twice to the hill – haircut for Mike & self - & it's now passing 11 o'clock & I've a shirt to iron for G & my dishes to wash. Haven't been anywhere since you left. The two airmen came up on Wednesday night – they couldn't find the house & had to get old Johnnie Eunson to bring them around – had quite a pleasant evening – played darts most of the time – left at 25 minutes to 2.

The next night the two Laurenson boys came up & played darts with Mike – finally managed to push them out at the back of eleven.

Friday night Babbie [*also Laurenson*] came up – Sat. clear – Sunday afternoon, Mary [*Williamson*] came in.

Today Titch came in just when we were finishing dinner – nice fried haddock.

Sent JM down to the pier today to see if he could buy some fish – Jimmie Williamson gave him three beauties – and when he asked the cost said – "These are to wish your faither luck" – very nice of him, wasn't it.

On Saturday JM got some roes & four scallops – gosh they were good – the scallops I mean.

Longing to get a letter & to hear all news – do take care of yourself. Give my love to the Scott family.

All my love, dear Christopher

the house seems very empty without you

Valda

PS
Enclosing U.E. form – letters from B. Fairley, V. Stewart & [*Council of*] C. Liberties

It's been snowing heavily since 2.30pm – quite a few inches of snow - & now I hear the wind rising

[*cont'd along side of page*] probably G[*torn*] not be able to get tomorrow.

Whalsay

16.2.42

My dearest Christopher,

Your letter came today – how glad I was to get it and to know things weren't going too badly with you – you sound very cheerful – but I know how irksome you must find it or will find it, say – once the newness has worn off.

I both laughed & cried – when I read of you – cutting the metal blocks with a hack saw – poor darling – I'd rather do it myself.

I'm glad you're at A.G.G.'s[102] it will certainly be more comfortable than in digs (at S–m[103] they push 6 in room – so Mary's lodgers were saying) & I was quite worried wondering how you would fare. It's a pity it is so far away. I hate the thought of your getting up at 5. am[104] – do take care of yourself – let yourself go when you write & don't be too cheerful otherwise I'll suspect things aren't as they should be.

Grant went last Tuesday & on the Wednesday a dreadful storm blew up – it had already been snowing for days & the wind blew the snow in great drifts – from the Bruce's brae to the Drs. The drifts were so high I couldn't see over the top. The roof of our dunnigan blew clean off during the night - & going for milk – the wind knocked me off my feet – what a cut knee I got – haven't had one like it since my schooldays. Coming up from the well I fell into a snowdrift & lost all my water – I cursed, laughed & lost my breath & had to go back & get more – the wind was terrific.

It's been quite mild today – thank goodness.

---

102 Andrew Graham Grieve, Christopher's brother, a widower since 2 years previous, at which time Christopher had written expressing condolences on the death of A. Graham's wife Chryssie, writing again very affectionately and sympathetically in March, by which time he had learned more of the circumstances of his sister-in-law's illness and death.

103 Valda's omission – no doubt a war-time precaution.

104 The shifts were 7am-1pm, 2-10pm and 10pm-6am and staying at Graham's meant "one has to be up and out an hour before the time the shift starts in order to clock in on time, which is of course essential....early shift means rising at 5 am..." (*NSL*, pp. 200-1).

People are complaining that I'm never seen these days – have been twice to Symbister since you left – been having the usual clear-up & have reached the back kitchen.

Yes! I'll send along the books to F.G.'s next week. I don't know where to look for the poem – unless it's in one of the books – anyway I'll have a good look through them.[105]

Have sent the money to Brand & Mollinson for your raincoat & told them to send it to you. How did you manage to get your dungaree's – do they provide them? Whatever you do – don't buy a cap – that would be the last straw. Will send your clothes by Friday's mail – if there is anything you need don't forget to let me know.

I'm enclosing a few letters – I thought of writing Cottons myself – but my second thoughts decided you'd better do it. I'm getting a form tomorrow to fill & see what can be done. I've looked up the dates the other two parcels (4 Oct.) were sent & should think the missing parcel was sent off about December.

[*letter ends in MS 27149 folder; cont'd. on folio p. 21, MS 27150, NLS.*]

I miss you an awful lot far more than I thought I would – and only hope this job of yours pans out in our favour for once. I'll hang on at this end & try & straighten things out a bit & be ready to come when you're fully fledged. I think we should seize the opportunity to get clear from here – I can't help you darling – the only person who can do that is yourself – but remember I love you quite a lot.

[105] *NSL*, p. 202, Christopher's letter of 10th February: 'There's just one thing I want you to do. You know the four volumes of old Scots poetry I got from that bookseller in Edinburgh. They are on the third or fourth shelf of my bookcase – the one at my right hand when I'm sitting on my chair. Well I want you to parcel them up, and along with them the pamphlet of your poem of Burns's we got once from Mary Shearer if you can find it – the one about twirling at the canister etc. – and send that parcel to F.G. Scott ... as soon as you can spare the cash to post it.'

I can't remember asking you to get anything but a dog's collar from Woolworths – nothing more expensive.[106]

Give my love to the Scotts & to Graham & family.

... Perhaps I should have forwarded Millars wire – but I hadn't bargained for the steamer to be four days late.

Have you had word from Mrs Watson yet?

I had a form to fill up from Thornliebank today – wanting a few particulars – mostly confirming your application I should think. A back payment arrived & as it was still made out to you I signed you named [*sic*] – old Mymie[107] changed it – I trust it is OK – anyway they won't be able to get it back that's one thing.

I don't suppose for one minute that you'll be able to decipher half of this horrible scrawl – "it's the pen that's wrong not me". Do you remember that song in the last war – "Paddy wrote a letter to his Irish Mollie – O" ?

It's dreadfully late – gone 1 am - & I'll have to be up early tomorrow to get this posted – how I hate getting up in the morning – I hope you get something to eat before you go out at that godless hour –

All my love

Valda

PS
How did you manage going down? You must have been very short.

---

[106] Christopher's letter of 10th February, cont'd.: ' P.S. I am haunted by an idea that there was something you wanted me to get you at Woolworth's or somewhere – or was it some hair stuff or something? Please let me know and I'll see to it immediately. Also if there are other odds and ends you want just tell me and I'll get them for you.'

[107] Jemima Nicolson, postmistress (*The New Shetlander, ibid*).

Thursday afternoon

[*19 February 1942*]

Dearest Christopher,

Just a scrawl to go with the parcel – letter proper – during the weekend – I'd sent JM up to the shop to get an ounce of tob. to go in parcel (you'll find it in huge socks) when your wire came – what a surprise - & how thankful (am paying rates pronto). Are you sure you're keeping enough for yourself? You must get yourself a pair of decent shoes very soon – now do that as soon as you can – won't you!

Will send volumes of[*f*] packing to Scott next mail & there hasn't been a South boat in for a fortnight - & no-one seems to know what has happened to her.

For Gods sake be careful in the black-out & if you cannot get refill for your torch let me know – you have one in your bag remember. Keep this box & paper it will do to send your laundry in.

The weather is very much milder & quieter – we need it. I'm still covered in "blue melts" as Mike calls it.

I'll have to hurry down to the post – it closes at 6pm & I have the dishes to wash. I'd a thousands times rather scrub six floors .

One good joke – when Mike brought the wire in I said – "I wonder what happened" – "Perhaps Daddy's been put in jail" – said your son. He's evidently got you taped.

Kindest regards to all the Grieves - & anyone else whom you may see –

Love

Valda

Wed. morning
[*25 February 1942*]
Sudheim
Whalsay
Shetland Isles

My dearest Christopher,

How glad I was to get your lovely long letter on Monday – the previous one was getting a bit scruffy through being read so often.

I meant to have got this off by the yesterday mail, but failed to get it done on Monday – I did a whole heap of letters on Monday afternoon – sent books to Scott posted Rates - & back payments to World's books. Just managed to get to the P.O. by 6 pm – had a long wait in Hays & arrived back for tea at 7.30 pm so that everything was gone – before I had a chance to look at.

Mike started school on Monday – it is still intensely cold & everywhere covered in snow. There's a rumour going round that the parents are going to keep their children home – being dissatisfied with the way they are being taught – or rather not taught. Yesterday Mike didn't do a thing (except sit by the fire) from the big play hour to the time for coming home. I don't suppose it will come to anything – you know what they're like.

The Home Guard – some 80 odd are doing wonders & shitting miracles – they had a rifle practice on Sunday – used some thousand bullets - & the only one who could hit the bull was young Magnie Hutchison (the house further along from Annies – Ina's brother he's only 16). They train in the hall – it's too cold on the [? *Wart*[108]] one night they had a mock alarm & had to fall out at 3 a.m. Smith's one of the officers & helps with the drill. What a bloody farce. The invasion of Shetland rumour is rife again. There's supposed to be a lot of activity in Norway just now – certainly a German plane is over most nights recently.

[108] A Shetland resident suggested 'Wart' – John Manson, corresp.

I bet you felt terribly bucked when you wired the dough[109] – for goodness sake take care of yourself. The Bulletin always full of people being killed stepping of[*f*] trams. You must be more careful.

It doesn't look as if you're going to get much time for your own work – which is the main thing – perhaps as you say once you get things taped properly you'll manage better.

Are all these hundreds of young men & women[110] prospective viewers & inspectors?

It will be splendid if you can see T.S. Eliot – I trust it comes off all right.

What word have you from Methuens – not good – otherwise you would have told me.

Had a great day baking yesterday – nutmeg flavoured buns, jam tarts, mince pies – wish you'd been here to share them – it's not half so much fun just baking for oneself.

Babbie, Lorena [*Laurina*] & Mary Shearer came in last night & gave me a hand with my gloves.[111] They got 3 prs done to the fingers (& I did a pair of kids') – they're giving 5/- for them here now.

JM & I had a poetry reading one night – he quite enjoyed it – by the way he thinks you write lovely letters. I think it would be good plan to wire the money every week. The cost isn't a great deal, is it? Not because I need it – but it reassures me that you're OK – Monday to Monday is a long time to wait & worry. I'm paying off the smaller debts but I'm also putting something aside each week – we'll be as careful as we can this end. Be sure & keep enough for your own wants – I'll send some matches when the next lot comes in.

---

109 'I wired you yesterday and sent some dough. I'd have sent more but had my out-of-pocket expenses to next payday to consider (about 6/- for bus and train charges and about the same for hot meal in works canteen at break half-way through shift).' – Christopher's letter of 20 February, *NSL*, p. 203.

110 Colleagues.

111 Valda learned to knit Fair Isle to selling standard.

Just going to make a cup of coffee & then go down & post this. I wait until JM comes home (3pm) for dinner. The steamer sailings have changed – up on Mondays down on Tuesday – up on Wednesday early – down in the afternoons up Friday down Saturday.

Stalin gave a fine speech to the Red Army & incidentally let our people know that he was only concerned with driving out the Nazi Germans from Russian territory - & that he had no intention of destroying the German people – how different from Churchill's Billingsgate display.

My kindest regards to all –

Cheerio dearest

all my love

Valda

PS If I send you some halibut oil capsules will you take them? They help night blindness etc

Sudheim
Whalsay
Tuesday
[*3 March 1942*]

My dearest Christopher,

Was awfully disappointed at not getting a letter from you on Monday. I trust everything is OK. There's a mail tomorrow so perhaps there will be a letter for me.

Thanks for wire received on Saturday.

What like is the weather in Glasgow. Here it is dreadful – we've had more snow - & a hard frost. The wind fairly high and piercingly cold.

Had a parcel of leeks from home yesterday. Wish you were here to have a share of the leek pie.

Is there such a thing as an Alladin [*sic*] Mantel No. 12 down your way – mine went phut about a week ago – have tried Lerwick – but can't get one & the Pifco is just a damned nuisance – I can scarcely see to write this.

Did you see T.S. Eliot? And have you heard any word from Methuens yet.

I had a letter from Dugald last week - & yesterday Rosita Forbes – *Russian Road to India*[112] – haven't read it yet only glanced through it & read a bit here & there – it seems good.

Made up one of your old evening shirts (the one with the cigarette burn) into a blouse for myself & dyed it very successfully daffodil yellow – it looks fine with the scarf Helen gave me a couple of years ago.

The papers still come from Dr Orr - & another bundle of Times Litts. [*Times Literary Supplements*]came from Helen – I'm sending them on.

Enclosing letter from Michael Roberts – cheque came for 10/6. Have sent for a pair of pyjamas for you from Pontings.

Now the rush of cleaning is over – I find it very lonely without you.

I'll wait until tomorrow to finish this in case there's a letter from you.

---

112 In Penguin series, published New York 1940.

Thule is waxing big & strong. Mike is very bucked – she was tethered outside Babbie's & he was going down to Hays for Babbie & took Winston with him – Thule chewed her tether & went after him – he's never ceased singing her praises.

Here is a poem by T.E. Nicholas – translated from the Welsh by David Raymond

America Calling

(President Roosevelt has telegraphed Stalin asking him about the position of religion in Russia – News Report)

I

"Joe
Tell me.
For there are people who demand to know
If priest and churches of your land
Are free as once they used to be
To minister religion for a fee?

II

Do you,
As happens here
Burn sacrificial wheat
Witheld from mouths
Forbidden by economic law
To eat?

III

Do you,
Like us,
to please the gods

and raise the price,
Burn cotton
Which could clothe the
Men who live on rice?

IV

And,
Say!
Do you lynch Negroes
In the name of Piety
Because they didn't know the laws of racial purity?

V

Is Brotherhood of man with you
Conditioned by skin and colour?
And prayer a mercenary wagging of the chin?

VI

Do tell me,
Joe, -
Have you the liberty of worship in your land?
The priest of Mammon here insistently demand.

—

Friday

Received your letter & wire today – many thanks, my darling. I'm dreadfully sorry you've such a beastly cold – I only wish you could have fallen for something easier – if we'd only gone the right way about it I think it could have been done. I hate to think of the strain it must put on you.

This intensely cold spell must be pretty general – they've had it in Cornwall – even the canal frozen – Aunt Jane has been ill - & all by herself. Aunt Agnes said she is very, very weak – can hardly move around yet has to get her work done.

Goodness only know[*s*] what this will be like I'm not writing by the aid of a candle & the little lamp the Pifco new glass & mantle went sailing through the air a couple of nights ago - & it wasn't for want of care – I lit the damned thing at 5.30 & it was nearly seven before I turn[*ed*] it up. I hope you can get an Addlan [*sic*] mantel for me. Have also sent to Cornwall – just in case you should have difficulty.

It was a pity you didn't manage to meet T.S. Eliot. Splendid! I'm glad you've been to the pictures & other things it must be really exciting seeing Scott again.

The parcel hasn't come yet – it's only about 8 pm – plenty of time for Dickie.

You mustn't bother to send me parcels. We manage none so badly up here – as you know.

There are hundreds of things I want to ask you that I really don't know where to begin. Michael was going to write you – but he's got a couple of Rovers – he thoroughly enjoyed "*The Kingdom that Was*" & "*The Return of Dr Syn*" – it's a *Cherry Tree* book. He'll be very glad of the Westerns – but don't go spending very much – you need it, old dear. How do you manage about smoking during the work hours?

My kindest regards to the Scotts and Morag & Graham – is Angus at home?

All my love
Valda

[*on reverse*]

PS A mine went off at about 4 am this morning what a fright we got – thought the Germans had landed the house shook & in the living room the plaster fell off the back wall – another went off about breakfast time – but it was further north so we scarcely felt it.

Enclosing letters from
Michael Roberts
Erik Schache
Mackies. Sending separately *Times Litts* & *Saltire News*

Sat. morning

Have you seen about your specs yet? I think they could be riveted – I know Midge had it done to hers. Do take all the care you can of yourself – Do I sound rather like a broody hen?[113]

Love V.

[113] Christopher had begun addressing Valda 'Dearest Hen-Bird' in his previous letter (20th Feb. '42).

Whalsay

15/3/42

Hello darling,

I've just enough energy left to scrawl a few lines – dear God the weather – it's awful – steamers all astray again – snow – gales & all the etc etc I could never weather a whole winter on my own I'd pass out.

Many thanks for the very nice parcel – which we received yesterday. Everything was good & it was awfully sweet of you.

Something has just gone off bang – another mine I expect – no doubt the Censors will cut this out – aren't they bloody fools.

This is being written by candlelight & it's a hell of a light – I'll send the books by the next post also several pairs of socks & a pair of pants – I think Mary has jammed the arse beautifully – don't you?

It is a black dirty night - & I trust you are not grubbing about in it – do take care of your dear self.

Thank Morag for the magazine – JM has thoroughly enjoy[*ed*] the Edgar Wallace. I'm reading "T*he Duke*" just now – that's the last of the Jamison lot – Gertie Halcrow has lent me *Potemkin* by George Soloveytchik. You will of course know of it – is it good or not?

No letter from you this past week – the one in the parcel didn't count it was written before your letter of March 1st. Received the wire on Friday – many thanks.

The kettle is just coming to the boil I'm going to make some tea & away to bed – it's just gone midnight. Have you been at the Scotts today I wonder.

I kept Mike home from school on Friday – he has a bad sty & came home from school with it very runny – now there is another one developing – being runned down after the whooping cough I expect is the cause.

Your departure to work in a munition factory was discussed in the Employment office in front of a Whalsay man – when confronted with it – I said "It's the first I've heard of it" - & left it at that.

I'm having a makin' as soon as I get my lamp fixed up – getting your vest underway & pants for Mike – trying hard to get everything in that line cleared up – because I'm not going to be too long away from you –

Goodnight

Love

Valda

Whalsay

27/3/42

My dearest one,

Many thanks for your lovely long letter of the 15th . Sorry my last was such a scrawl but I was simply just all in – we're having dreadful weather still – a heavy fall & snow earlier in the week – it's just too bad.

We've had no South steamer for a fortnight – she's in now I believe, but of course the *Earl* didn't wait for the mails this morning - rather too much I expect – so I haven't got the mantles yet.

Thanks for wire received on Wednesday afternoon – was damned glad to get it – thought something must have happened to you & was worrying.

I'm coming down to you as soon as I can - & I'm not going down to Cornwall – we'll stay together wherever you go – maybe we could get JM evacuated – it's hardly fair to keep him near a munitions works. Mrs MacCarthur [*sic*] takes evacuees doesn't she – perhaps she would take him until we see how we're fixed. Write & ask her – will you? [114] I will pack all the books in the wardrobe – let me know of any you wish to have with you. Blankets, sheets etc I'll need – I could send them down in driblets – perhaps Helen would store them for me – all this of course will take me a couple of months or more for I simply can't start a thing until it gets warmer – been working like the devil on my blanket & have almost finished it – it's really handsome.

Now darling think things over & talk it over with F.G. – I really cannot stay up here without you, so shall I just go picking things up quietly & get ready?

I've paid the Rates – and one or two small items – Mallie for 2 months milk – a few things in the Black Book - & *New Directions* £2 – to Johnnie Shearer[115] – I pay something every week & the smaller things will soon get squared. Let me know next time you write what you think about things.

[114] Editors of the *New Selected Letters* point out this is Bessie J B MacArthur, Scottish poet (p. 216).

[115] Butcher.

I sent off a parcel last week & will try & get the other one off tomorrow – I meant to have had another pair of socks ready, but couldn't manage it.

I'm glad you're having an interesting time – but do take care of yourself I love you quite a lot, you know.

There isn't much news here of course. The kids are having a weeks holiday starting from today. [...] is supposed to be enceinte[116] – about 4 months – so the wise women say – rotten luck if it's true.

I forgot to mention Dugald was bellyaching in his last letter at not hearing from you – must answer it – I haven't done so yet or he'll have hot grouses.

Mollie's Laura has been called up – she[*'s*] gone in [*to a*] munitions down in England – working a machine – says there's nothing in it.

Have you got to do all the things you're doing to become an inspector or viewer or are you just an ordinary M. worker?

Mike's cough is pretty bad still & he gets awfully tired – of course he takes far too much out of himself – the other day he cycled right round the island by himself after school & was very bucked with himself – too much for him – all the same.

It's 12.30 all ready & I must try & get your parcel done up – please save all the brown paper & string – I'm very hard up in this line.

I wonder if you'll meet Paul Potts – it must be a treat to meet humans once more after so long with the stones & the beasts.

The fire is going down & it's getting chilly – write soon darling.

all my love
Valda

PS Try & get the comb, will you?

---

[116] Strictly speaking, approx. 6 months pregnant – Valda uses here the same word Christopher had used in London when he had been proud to announce to their friends she was pregnant with James Michael. 'Christopher was so enthusiastic. Every time we'd go into a pub he would announce for all to hear – "Valda's enceinte – did you know that?" God, I was shocked!' – Valda's interview with Raymond Ross for *Scotsman* article of 1 September 1984.

Sudheim

2/4/42

My dearest Christopher,

It's getting on for one o'clock – and I should be getting some beauty sleep. And how!

Thanks so much for the parcels of books & letters received on Monday – your letters had quite a glad note – I'm glad for your sake as well as my own that things are looking a little brighter for us – also that outside your work you are finding things stimulating. Wish I'd been at the meeting.[117] Doesn't Archer mix with the crowd that tried to do you in? Be careful old dear — .

I really should have answered per return because by now you will have got my letters & will be thinking that I'm going to land myself down on you at any moment – don't worry it will take me months of hard work to get everything shipshape for if I'm going to be away for any length of time everything will have to be carefully packed away. As long as I'm away before the winter sets in – for I simply couldn't manage a winter on my own. These past weeks have nearly floored me. Yesterday it was bitterly cold & we had a fall of snow – but today has been lovely – the first bit of sunshine for the year.

A mantel turned up from Cornwall, thank God.

Mike has been in with another sty – an awful looking thing – he still coughs badly at night & easily gets upset.

He's been reading a bundle of Readers' Digest he got from Robert John. Today he told me his potatoes were lovely – he swathed them in sauce.

I expect tonight you will be meeting Paul Potts.

---

[117] Christopher wrote he'd spoken for over 2 hours at The Centre, "David Archer's literary and artistic rendezvous." "The meeting began at 8pm and it was midnight before I got back to Cambuslang. I enjoyed it immensely and so did the audience. It was a very lively crowd of literary and artistic people and keen Scottish Nationalists and Communists and I was at the very top of my form. Amongst those present were many friends of mine I hadn't seen for years..." (*NSL*, p. 211).

I've found the Burns poem & will send it on to F.G.

What a blessing it must be to be off the night shift & how thankful you must be for the lighter nights and it will be better soon with the extra hour.

Do you want another battery for your torch? By the way did you ever get your raincoat?

I've read quite a bit of the Nonsense Verse – Lewis Carroll more than holds his own. I enjoyed "*Russian Road to India*" (Dugald sent it) the scenic descriptions have an interest of their own – while the confessions she is sometimes forced to make – in spite of herself – is of still greater interest and importance.

There was quite a lot I wanted to say – but I'm afraid it will have to wait until next time – otherwise I'll never be up in time to get this posted. You know what I'm like.

Thanks for the £s received last week – I didn't get any the week before – is that right? Forgive my mentioning it – I was quite OK but from something you said in your letter I thought perhaps you had wired me and that it was wiser to mention it. Now don't go reading into this something that isn't there – you should know me better by this time.

I'm almost falling asleep.

Goodnight my dearest & thank you for your lovely long letters –

All my love

Valda

Whalsay

10/4/42

My dearest Christopher,

I meant to write you a long letter tonight but Babbie came up and now it's gone midnight. Michael wrote you earlier in the evening while I was washing up the dishes – must read it before I enclose for I expect it will be some epistle. What lovely things you sent him and he is some bucked I can tell you – the bell arrived on Monday and the knife & mantle on Wednesday – many thanks.[118]

By the way I've been up inspecting the cottage (the first week we've had minus snow since you left) and I think the sooner it is off our hands the better otherwise we'll be sued for repairs. It was in a terrible state – I've rescued all your MSS & letters (3 suitcases full – I was cursing by the time I'd dragged them home) & I wonder what I'd better do about the news papers a lot of them are beyond repair I'm afraid – and even if I dried them I don't see they'd be much use – for even if things go well – it will be years before you can do anything with them & by that time I expect you'll be wanting to write something very different – especially if we manage to survive this war.

The *Modern Scot*'s & pamphlets I'll get down but won't touch the newspaper, *Picture Post*, *New York Nations* & *Times Litt.* until I hear from you.

I've put all your MSS in one tea box & your letters in another – both from the cottage & upstairs – so they're as safe as I can make them. Also put your newspapers in tea boxes (3 boxes of them & if I could only throw away the *News of the World*s – I'd probably do with far less). Now don't get up in the air – it's the only thing I can do under the circumstances.

What I really think would be the wisest plan would be to get rid of this place at the end of the summer & when you get settled down – I feel sure we could make enough to clear ourselves here & pay our fare down. I know if it is left for any length of time it will decay rap-

[118] Christopher had been trying since arrival in Glasgow to find a bicycle bell for Michael as well as the lamp mantles Valda had requested.

idly – for it is so damp (chew your cud over this) and we'll lose the few sticks we have in it - & half the value of the house.

Of course all this depends on if you get a job - & as you say nothing must be done in a hurry – but if we can decide what we're going to do – I can go about clearing things up to that end – the mere thought of it appal[*l*]s me, but if I know in good time I think I can manage.

But let me know re the cottage papers per return – I bet you're sweating blood.

Will answer other things in your letter during the weekend – excuse this hasty scrawl I really shouldn't of broached the subject tonight – but felt I had to get it off my chest. If we did decide to leave here I could send your 2 tea boxes down to Orr – of course we'd have to ask him first. Mary would store the books – expect [*except*] a few that we really need.

Mike has been home from school today – he's been complaining of pains in his side & chest – he's certainly far from well.

I have found your chapter "*A Ride on a Neugle*"[119] & would have enclosed it – but I'll need to registered [*sic*] it - & can't afford it this week – sorry to mention it, but it's a fortnight since I had any dough & I'm almost on the rocks – had to borrow a few shillings from JM.

Take care of your dear self. Tell me all about Paul Potts and did you see Orr? Finished my blanket today – a blessed relieve [*sic*] also finished the peats at the house & started to stack on the hill.

Trust there will be a letter from you on Monday – they seem to take ages coming.

The fire is out & I'm beginning to shiver –

All my love, dearest
Valda

Fraid there are a lot of mistakes – but the little grey cells refuse to work at this hour

119 From Christopher's autobiography.

[*on Christopher's printed notepaper, and torn*:]
from hugh macdiarmid
(C.M. GRIEVE)
WHALSAY
VIA LERWICK
SHETLAND ISLANDS]

[*April 1942*]

My dearest Christopher,

I want to get this letter written before Mary Shearer comes in – otherwise it will have to wait until Saturday & that is rather a long time.

Many thanks for your letter received yesterday and wire received today. Splendid darling.

I'm glad Paul Potts turned out to be such a decent fellow (often one is disappointed over letter friendships) & that you all had a stirring weekend. I'm pleased you saw Orr. Do you ever see the Scotts now? Or have the new friends cut them out. And that reminds me a bitter lecture is due on my part. I simply cannot go three weeks without any money (it will be 3 weeks tomorrow) and I think you should realise that. I note what you say about "being in Rome one has to some extent do as Rome does" – there is also another one — to cut one's suit according to one's cloth – and that is what we've to do just now so for goodness sake be your age and know when to say no.

For a long time – we'll have to go extremely carefully – you know that and this is a chance I'm sure for us to get on a better footing financially. I'm doing my bit this end & it's a damned rough end of the stick I can tell you – and I want you to do yours – for god's sake don't run up any more bills – I'm sick of the sight of them – let's try & start with a clean sheet for a change.

I've been thinking things over very carefully – weighing all the pro's & con's & have come to the conclusion that the best & wisest course for me to do is to get [*page torn*] of this place & its contents [*tear*] I would then be able to square [*tear*] due here & probably pay my [*tear*] fare – I do not purpose [*sic*] landing myself on you as immedia[*tely*] a little fling away from domestic ties won't hurt you

- & in any case we must try & save a bit before I venture forth – I'll have a hell of a difficult & hard time of it – I will need a rest & holiday before I start in again. After that I may even take a job myself. Laura says it's child's play just turning a handle.

All your MSS I've packed in a tea box – are the typescripts of *Scottish Eccentrics & the Islands*[120] books of any use? Let me know. I've been through the letters & discarded all empty envelopes bills & *bumming* letters – these ammounted [*sic*] to nearly 2 tea boxes full I'm lighting fires with them.

The books I can deal with – some I'll take with me others I'll leave with Mary Shearer. Your newspapers are the problem – certainly we cannot take the whole lot – yet some without others aren't much use either. So what am I to do. Mary hasn't room for anything more than the books – she said she'd room for 3 tea boxes & that's all.

This may seem very callous – lack understanding & what not – this is our chance to get clear of this place & it's not going to be my blame if we don't – you've often blamed me for our coming up here but you won't be able to say I didn't try to get out. You may think it's early days to be making plans but I have to plan ahead – it will be damned hard work & I have to do it all myself & I'm not exactly in the peak of condition. Please take time off from your various activities to answer this fully.

Sorry if this isn't a very nice letter – but I'm not feeling too good tempered. JM has been in bed for 3 days poor little chap with a dreadful chest cold & cough he's had a temperature & talking queer I really thought I'd have to call the Dr in – also I hadn't a bean & had to borrow money to post this from Mary.

Have you written Mrs MacArthur yet? I wish you would.

I was quite excited to get your wire this morning I trust it is something & somewhere you like – shall be very impatient until I hear.

120 *The Islands of Scotland: Hebrides, Orkneys and Shetlands* (London: B.T.Batsford Ltd., 1939).

Thank you very much for the books I'll enjoy them I know – but please don't send me any more – I know it all cost money as you say & I really have plenty to read & won't get much time for reading unfortunately for some time to come. I'm knitting vests for you at the moment & they are quite a hefty piece of work. Your pyjamas have come from Ponting. I bought those with Michael Robert's cheque. The American cheque was for £2 – 14-9 I paid £2 to J. Shearers & paid Arthur's 19/5 I had in the books – so you see I got nothing from them in fact I had to add to them.

I think it would be a very good idea to get Michael a suit – a size 8 is what to ask for – it's a bit big but he wouldn't want to wear it for a little while. I'm enclosing a sheet of coupons – use these first for anything you need as they are cancelled in May.

Would you get me 8 ozs Paton & Baldwins 4 ply super fingering in Navy please.

And would you ask Morag [*tear in page*] I could send on a cardboard box [*tear*] clothes that I won't need here. I'll mark it & let you know before hand that I'm sending it – there will [*be*] no need to undo it as long as [*tear*] is kept somewhere dry.

Sorry this is such a [*b*]ad-tempered scrawl – but it's been [*b*]itterly cold today & sitting up in Grant's [*room*] – wading through those letters [*is*] enough to try anyone's patience.

All my love

Valda

Tuesday 27th
Midnight
[*Tuesday 28 April 1942*]

My dearest Christopher,

It was cheering to get your long short[121] letter yesterday but I'm very unhappy to think of you working 14 hours a day & cannot see how you can keep going without cracking up – just our bloomin' luck that you should land a job like that. When I get down we'll get a place near the works & then that will cut out all the time involved in travelling.

I'm bucked to the skies to think of Michael having a chance at last[122] – for I feel very responsible for him & I'm truely [*sic*] grateful to you for thinking of him. I haven't said anything to him about it yet – for I feel sure he could not keep that to himself, but told him he could take Thule down - & his face lit up – when I came to the bit in your letter about giving the newspapers to the salvage company – he said – "It's a great sacrifice for him."

It will take me a couple of months at least to get things packed up – it's only a one-man show - & will take some doing. I shall try & pay the rent during May & will give up my lease of the Harlsdale Cottage give the newspapers away & keep *Modern Scots* & pamphlets – that is clear isn't it?

Here I send as many things by post as possible household linen – and all clothes. All furniture I sell – and the compensation for the house. Also I don't think I need load myself up with crockery (except the China teaset) we'll always be able to get enough for our modest needs. Let me know if you approve. I wish I could manage to pay Johnnie Georgie the £15 we owe him - & then I'd be clear of him & be able to deal with any applicants for the house myself – otherwise I can forsee endless trouble – you know what these

121 Christopher had written, "This is only to be a short letter in order to avoid too long a gap…." (*NSL*, p. 223).

122 The proposal is that Michael attend Kilquhanity School, "the only really good experimental school in Scotland….not only run on lines which [*Christopher feels*] certain Michael will enjoy immensely but which will be very good indeed for his development…" (*NSL* p. 225).

people are like – they won't know [?*how*] to see about it. I'll put a spurt on my knitting & see what I can do this end – for I think I'll come off the better if the house is cleared.

All your MSS are packed in a teabox & letters in another. What am I to do with the newspapers in Grants room? What books would you like me to bring down?

I shall bring – your own works - & my Lawrence collection & a few others.

I'm sending a parcel of blankets tomorrow – there is nothing in the parcel for you so if it is easier for Morag to keep them parcelled up just don't open them up – any parcel I send addressed to C. M. Grieve, Esq. you'll know contains only stuff I'm sending down to store – all others intended for you will be addressed Christopher Grieve – savvy!

The weather has really been lovely – but I've been feeling "wappit" out – one day my tummy bothers me – another my legs ache as if they were coming off – the next it's my head, or the back of my neck - & in consequence I'm not getting much done.

Walter Robertson[123] very kindly came over & offered to cut our peats again this year – so he's coming tomorrow to cut the big upper bank – I didn't want to tell him I wouldn't need them.

Grant arrived unexpectedly last Tuesday – got compassionate leave - [...]. Grant is probably leaving here on Saturday & is going to try & see you when he passes through Glasgow.

Will leave this over until tomorrow there may be other news by the post – take care of yourself my dear one – for I'm longing to be with you again.

Love

Valda

[123] This was the Whalsay man, interested in poetry, who had tried his best to teach Christopher how to cut peats.

Wednesday

In desperate haste to catch steamer – Walter arrived for peat cutting this morning & had to knock us up – what a blow! It wouldn't have happened if you'd been here.

Whalsay

7/5/42

My dearest Christopher,

Received your letter & Western today – you poor darling what a dreadful time you must have had – but I'm so glad you're being well looked after – don't bother about overtime – it isn't worth it – just you rest as much as possible.

This is only a short note – to catch the steamer as she goes down. I should have written last night – but I fell asleep in from of the fire and awaken cold & stiff. Grant is going today – he's taking a case down with him for you & if he doesn't see you will leave it at the Central Station & post you on the receipts.

I note all you say in your letters & will do my best – as you know – I'm sorry that anything has to be thrown away.

I've sorted out the papers in the other cottage - & kept a good few of the Pamphlets but a lot I discarded – old *Decachords*[124] etc. & some guide books. The London *Mercurys* I thought of giving to Walter – there's some good stuff in them but one has to be ruthless in these circumstances. The *Modern Scots* I've kept do you want "*The Hound & Horn*" - ?

Don't be in too much hurry to get a place – I'll give you the word when I'm about half way through – then you can set about it.

Could I get the other cottage cleared out & scrubbed & Grants room & your stuff packed up – then I can get ahead more quickly.

Re your pyjamas – I have them here - & the *Neugle* chapter. Have been hanging on to make up a parcel & register it on to you – have a pair of socks made up out of some odd navy wool I had lying by. Will send it on next week without fail. *New Direction* arrived end of last week – it's a splendid book – over 600 pages. I don't care much

124 *The Decachord : A Magazine for Poetry-Lovers*, edited by Philippa Hole, some editions edited by John Arnell; founded 1924. Hugh MacDiarmid is listed as a contributor.

for the American poetry – included some of the translation from the Russian aren't bad – but I've an idea they could have been better.

Now dearest I must stop & get Grant a bite before he goes. JM was glad of the Western & sends you his love. How many cigs did you send me? 10 came in a twenty packet & the parcel was torn at the end. Many thanks I'm just enjoying a good tuck in.

Of course I understand about the "doing" - don't you overdo things – will write longer letter next week –

All my love

Valda

PS
Enclosing letter from Sam MacLean

Shall I dispatch your MSS to Orr – it would be less expensive I should think than coming across country to Glasgow – he could fetch them from the steamer & run them up to us once we got settled in.

Whalsay
Wednesday 25th
[*?Wed. 27 May 1942*]

My dearest Christopher,

Many, many thanks for your lovely long letter – how glad I was to get – for it seems an age since I last heard from you and I was wondering & worrying – as usual.

Received wire on Saturday for which I was thankful – thankful for what it was worth – but more thankful for the message.

So the row has come at last – I'm not in the least surprised – you'll be far happier with the Scotts.[125]

I've written you one maybe two snotty letters for which I'm always sorry once they are posted – I don't think you've received them yet judging by your own letter my only excuse is that I was worried – the weather bitterly cold (& still is) & having no money & being bummed by this one & that – they sort of know I'm leaving without being told – you know how they ferret things out – so I was feeling pretty miserable.

Anyway I've paid Mollie[126] up for 4 months milk that brings me to Sept. – and paid the Arthurs for things I had in the "black book" about 10 days worth. I want to try & clear up something each week, then when I sell my stuff I'll have it to myself & be able to pay a fiver to Hays & Johnnie & still have a good bit left. I reckon they'll be quite nasty up above – the Arthurs I mean – I believe JM's Rubber shoes have gone down.

I have 3 tea boxes packed – with your papers & MSS from Grant's room – I[*'ve*] written Orr & asked him if I could send them on to him – haven't had time for a reply yet I think it would be cheaper that way.

---

125 Christopher had written to Valda on 21 May 1942 saying he'd had "a hell of a row with Graham – on politics. he is extremely reactionary and hates the working classes." (*NSL*, p. 229).

126 Mollie Irvine (née Moar) – John Manson, article in *The New Shetlander*.

I sent off a parcel last week – containing *New Directions* & your summer clothes – also a registered letter by last post containing Burns' "[?*Country Lassie*]" – the *Ride on the Neugle* – 2 American letters - & a letter from Walter de la Mare. I'm glad Grant didn't lose the bag – I was worried over the damned thing.

I'll send parcels to Scotts in future & the same arrangement stands – C M Grieve store somewhere – Christopher Grieve you will know it's for you to open.

I'll be able to get on much faster now that your papers are sorted up – it's taken such an age – I've gone through every paper to see if there is any mention of ballet – doctors – medicine etc.

This week I'll clean up the other cottage & try & get some of the parcels off that I've already got packed up. That will make a big clearance.

I'm just longing to be with you again & hope things will pan out OK for a good holiday together.

Here['s] hoping, love

Valda

My kindest regards to all the Scotts.

Re jumper I'll try – but won't promise they're all bunged up with private orders & very expensive – I couldn't get any for Annie Henning – for love or money. Is it ordinary lady's size?

Whalsay
1 June [*1942*]

My dearest Christopher,

The weather here is hellish – can't get on with any thing. Today received letter from Dugald & he says you are looking extremely well – I'm glad – he was very particular to stress re. your talk in the Central Hotel – that you drank these gingers – [?*hells*] truth – I won't know you. I was going to have a big night to-night – packing - with the assistance of an ex Welsh miner – he's a driver in the RAF camp & hates it like hell – you know they rather look down [*on*] him – but at about 7 pm it started to rain & its rained & is still pouring cats & dogs – Bad luck!

The weather has really been awful for the past month.

When next you write please give me the address of the Scotts laundry. I will have to send the clothes on the bed there – for I'll be needing it up to the last minute.

Despite the fact Mike's been away such a lot he was top again in the exams 147 marks – against Mary Jeans 128.[127] He only had 8/50 for sums – none right – but 2 marks for each one attempted.

Enclosing two letters. Fraid there isn't much news & I don't seem to have made much progress with the packing when the muddle is cleared up a bit – expect I'll find I've done quite a bit – if we could only get a nice warm day – I'd be able to wash the mats & get them dried & packed away. I managed to do the wool rug & one of the upstairs ones between the showers, but it's so much easier when one can just go ahead & slog at it.

Goodnight my darling. Sorry for this unsatisfactory letter – but I'm almost asleep – wish to God I was on the boat.

All love
Valda

[127] Christopher's reply of Monday, 15 June 1942 (in which he has to break the news he & other men from the Mond Nickel factory were suddenly dismissed a fortnight previously – he had been unable to bring himself to give this news sooner): "I am extremely proud of Mike's success in again being first prize winner. Kiss him from me and tell him how glad I am and how anxious to see him and determined by hook or crook that he will have the chance he deserves." *NSL*, p. 229.

Sudheim
Tuesday night
[*23 June 1942*]

My dearest Christopher,

I did not write over the weekend, because I really did not know what to say – received your wire on Thursday and I'm feeling dreadfully worried, wondering what on earth has cropped up to alter our plans. I only hope it does not mean I'm hung up here much longer – both for your sake and mine. I want to get away quickly.

Perhaps there will be a letter tomorrow – will add to this if there is – but I won't be able to answer it fully as the steamer goes back early in the afternoon – but all letters have to be posted by 1 pm because the P.O. closes – half holiday – you know I'm going to the Pictures tomorrow night and a Talkie at that – the Forces are having a Picture show down in the hall – have even had the electric laid on for the purpose & the public are invited – admission free – Christ! What a waste of money.

Michael is some excited – he's never seen a picture before – he's been home from school again with a couple of sties or is it stys?

The weather is hellish – just like the middle of winter. Haven't done more packing since I got your wire – have quite a few parcels ready for posting once I get some dough. What a bloomin' life. Don't for God's sake say I'm going to be stuck up here for another decade – for I know we'll both regret it

Wednesday morning

No letter this morning – do trust everything is OK.

All my love

Valda

Sudheim
Whalsay
26/6/42

My dear Christopher,

I was hoping to get a letter from you today – not in answer to mine I know you wouldn't have had time for that.

By your silence I gather things are just as bad – poor darling what in the hell are we going to do – I can't live up here on air - & you can't either.

I trust you will agree to my suggestions in my last letter & that you have already written to Mrs MacArthur – things are too desperate to let any chance go by – for the past two weeks we've been on very short rations & I'm down to my last shilling. My ex-miner provided a few extras otherwise the cupboard would have been bare – also cobbled my only pair shoes which were badly needing repairs.

I must try & borrow something from Mary Shearer next week if nothing come[*s*] in – it's awful up here – I can't even go out & earn a little. I feel sure if I came down I could get a job of some kind so for goodness sake try and arrange something for Michael & as soon as you have I'll come down – it's already out that I'm leaving & I confirmed it. I'm sorry to harass you when you are so worried & down – but it is essential that I should get down as quickly as possible – for our sakes.

Michael has been home from school all this week with two dreadful "styes" on his eye – the worse I've ever seen – even his face has swollen & sore. The school broke up today. He was disappointed at not being able to go for his prize.

Thule is whelping somewhere around the 22nd July.

I've had an offer for the house.

I wonder where I can send on my orange sea chest. I've my crockery packed in it and I do not want too much luggage to look after on my way down – it will be bad enough as it is I expect.

Sorry darling this isn't a very helpful letter but I can't help feeling like a rat in a trap & I do wish you had written – even two or three lines.

Have enclosed letter from Ratter – I thought you'd cleared the matter up – of course I didn't give him your address.

All my love

Valda

Kindest regards to all friends

POSTCARD

Christopher Grieve
c/o Scott,
44, Munro Road
Jordanhill
Glasgow Scotland

Whalsay
1/7/42

Many thanks for letter – received this morning – will write fully end of week. Trust things go all right – feeling very relieved – What a bloomin' life. Hellish weather here – more like November. Let me know where I can send orange sea chest in Glasgow – as it contains crockery & it's not much use sending it to Orr. Also if I can send some parcels of clothes to No 44 – or if they will be going away soon.

My love to all –

Valda

Can't realize I'm really leaving here soon - .

Friday night

[? *3 July 1942*]

Dearest Christopher,

Very sorry my last letter was so bad tempered – forgive me – my dear won't you? But you know how bloody bad tempered one can get up here what with JM being ill & not feeling too grand myself (have been getting nasty pains in my tummy for some time now) – I sometimes feel like flaying someone or other.

JM received the Westerns today – he was very bucked indeed. Don't send me any more I'll have enough to pack up as it is – received three today from World's Book Club – I was beginning to think they'd gone out of existence.

I'm going to give up smoking – just out of spite – I think it's hellish – don't you?

I wonder if you will still be in Glasgow – longing to know all about it – will have to be patience [*sic*] & wait until Monday or even Wednesday. If I could only get on the phone to you.

By the way – what is happening to your washing? It's time I was having some pants to wash and it's time you got a pair of shoes – instead of threatening to get a pair. I'm going to get JM a navy gabardine raincoat it will serve as a coat too – they're very dear 38/6 – but he must have something for coming down. I'm getting it with my glove money sending off some next week. Haven't been able to manage many this time can't get settled down.

We have had lovely weather for the last 3 days – but we're all feeling overcome with the sudden warmth – it was so unexpected —

All my love

Valda

Sudheim

6/7/42

My dear Christopher,

Was so glad to get your letter this morning - & to know things are looking a bit brighter. I wish you could get the Rolls Royce job – it would be much easier for you physically. Even if the money shouldn't be quite as much, I think it would be worth it in the end. Thank goodness you are nearer your work – that must be a blessing.

I'm worried, how you will manage when the Scotts are away. I'm sure you won't look after yourself properly – how will you get your rations? I think you should leave your book at the shop or get them to deliver it for you to the house – explain that you're working & can't get during shop hours.

I'll send on the orange (sea chest) box soon. Will let you know when it's on the way.

Have a large quantity of parcels done up to send on – but have been stuck for want of cash. Once those are cleared up & the books packed I'll have made some headway.

Please don't send me anything for my birthday – I'd rather you didn't I'll get something when I come down. What JM wants most is a book called "*The Three Commanders*" W.H.G.Kingston. Blackie & Son Ltd. put it out in a cheap edition 2/0 – or 2/6. He would be some pleased with it.

later

Have just been out for a walk with Thule & am drenched to the skin – had to change everything.

I'm sending on small parcel by this mail – just store it – there is nothing in it for you.

Will try & send you some eggs when I get some dough – they will help eke out your rations.

Have you ascertained yet from Graham whether Angus collected case from booking office – you should do so – as it contained a lot of things you valued —

"*Opus C- - - - - - - - -.*" (can't spell it) & Power's book of names to you & other things. Also you never said if you received the *Neugle* & the Burns' Poem.

What about the Alladin Lamp – shall I sell that too? Let me know.

Had a letter from David Shearer – Solicitor – re £2-8-0 due to Grantfield stores – if not paid by the end of the month a summons will be served. Once you get your regular pay we should be able to manage it. –I've borrowed a bit from Mary – just to keep going – but if I get something regular every week from you I should be able to save that amount - & to pay it up.

What about your laundry while the Scotts are away – will you send it to me – or get it done. By the way I hope you are wearing your summer pants – I sent them to Grahams address – before I knew you had left. Re wool for Mrs Scott – fraid it is while nigh impossible for me to get it – I can't get any myself – I could possibly get some fawn by buying sheeps wool & getting it exchanged – but the <u>coloured</u> wools are scarce & they wouldn't sell me enough to make a jumper anyway I'll see what I can do.

The three tea boxes I wish to send on to Orr – contains your newspapers (2 boxes) & 1 box of MSS.

I'm still packing books – dear God – I can see no end to them. Don't laugh have had a bout of poetry reading just lately. I read to my ex-miner when he comes down – we've done a lot of yours - & all the Welsh poetry I could lay hands on. Francis Adams – now we're doing Burns. I'm glad you're not here to hear my accent.

Mike was very envious – when I read him the bit about George & Malcolm cycling off to Taynuilt.

'Fraid this letter is very scrappy – I really have quite a lot to say – but can't get it out – that the worse of being so inarticulate.

It was very nice of you to remember my birthday – I did not remind you when I wrote last – altho' it was on my birthday (July 1st). –anyway it's just as nice – in fact better than a present – to know you remembered about it – .

Cheerio for now darling
All love
Valda

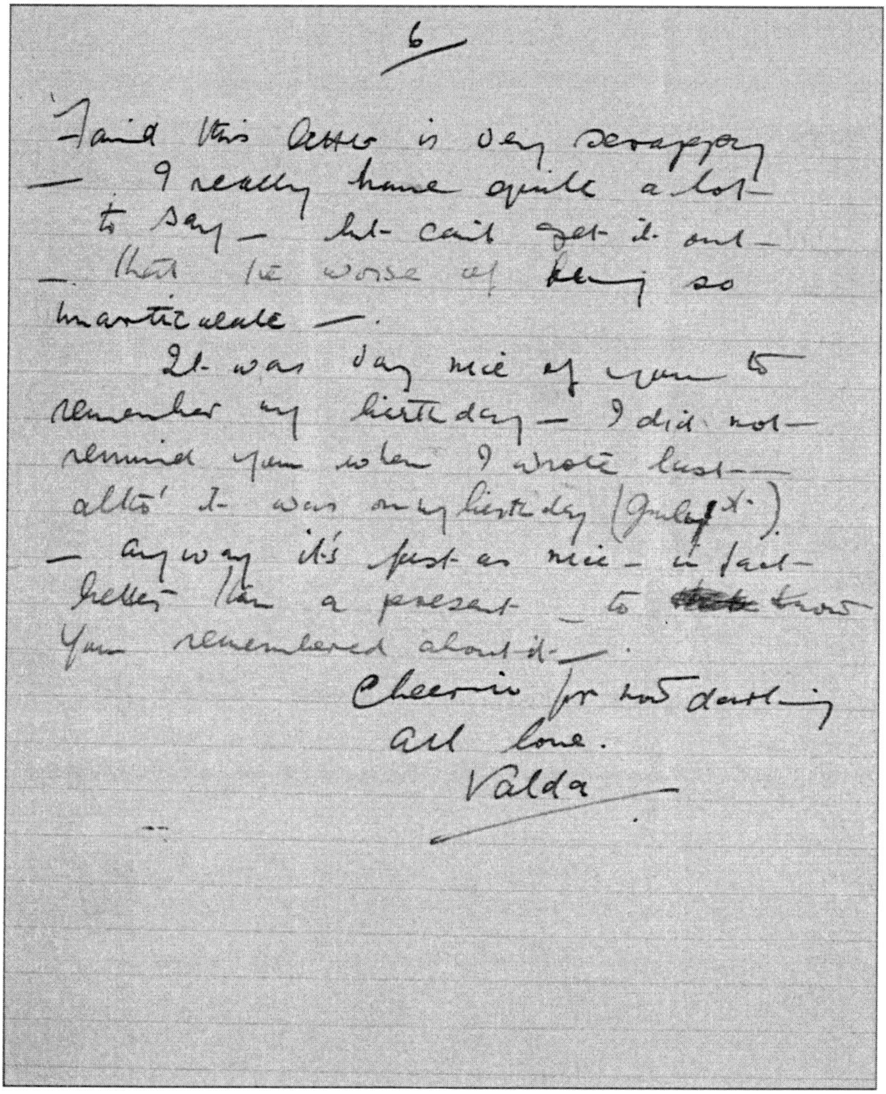

6

I fear this letter is very scrappy — I really have quite a lot to say — but can't get it out — that's the worse of being so inarticulate —.

It was very nice of you to remember my birthday — I did not remind you when I wrote last — altho' it was on my birthday (July 1st.) — anyway it's just as nice — in fact better than a present — to ~~[illegible]~~ know you remembered about it —.

Cheerio for now darling
All love.
Valda

Sudheim
Whalsay
15/7/42

My dearest Christopher,

I was so glad to get your letter this morning - & now I'm in a desperate hurry to get this down before 1 pm. I should have started it last night, but by the time I'd got Mike to bed – it was too dark to see anything – the days are drawing in rapidly now – it's too dim to do anything by midnight.

Mike is very bucked at the thought of getting the "T*hree Commanders*" – and there is no need to tell you how much – or how I feel – at the thought of getting "*The Cornish Heroic Song*" – it was a lovely thought on your part. Thank you Christopher. Always remember whatever happens I love you and only you – and could have shown & been so very much more if you'd only let me.

Thank goodness the men are decent with whom you're working – what a difference from the crowd up here – you could never have worked with them. Could you?

For goodness sake take care of yourself - & get as much rest as you can during your weeks holiday. I'll be glad to be with you again.

Yes! Black's brother-in-laws café is good. Dugald & I went there several times.

Are you sure it will be alright to send on my big <u>sea-chest</u> to the Scotts – goodness only knows how they'll get it inside the door. There isn't anywhere else I could send it is there.

Have you heard from Orr yet – about the tea-boxes? Or about what we're going to do with Mike?

Some people are "peeing" their breeks at the thought of my leaving – greedy buggers – but I'm holding my own so far - & won't turn them over to you until they're beyond my control.

I hear the smallpox is bad in Glasgow[128] – trust it doesn't spread. Had a letter from Mrs Scott today re wool – so will write her.

There is a Peter Davis down in the camp from Montrose – he knows of you well – he was an insurance agent among other things in Montrose. He was telling Babbie what a strong speaker you were - & how like you Michael was. I've seen him – but haven't spoken to him yet.

Wil[*l*] have to close now – with more than half unsaid – it's just on 1pm – but Mike will probably catch the post if he hurries on his bike – it's half day today.

All my love dearest

Valda

PS
I have not received your letter with the 15/ - yet.

What a pity – because you would probably have been glad of it - - and I know I would love it that time. Many thanks for the wire. Whew! What a blessed relief it was —

V.G.

How nice meeting Dylan Thomas & his wife.

[128] The Scottish outbreak of Smallpox in 1942 seems to have originated from a Glasgow ship-borne case and was transferred from area to area "by some means which careful investigation did not reveal." – '*The Edinburgh Outbreak of Smallpox 1942*', City of Edinburgh Public Health Department, a paper kindly sent to me by Norman MacDonald of the Scottish Centre for Infection and Environmental Health. The paper records the first case of City infection in Glasgow 23rd June, the last case recorded 31st July; first admission to a Glasgow hospital 26th June, last admission 31st July. It did spread, to Edinburgh.

Sudheim

27/7/42

My dear Christopher,

No letter from you last week – so I rather expected one today – but was disappointed – it's not awfully wise to neglect your wife – you know – even if she's middleaged.

It's JM's birthday tomorrow – he's got a nice pair of navy shorts from his Aunt Jane & a equally nice shirt from Aunt Agnes. I've got him a nice navy gaberdine raincoat – it came today – he's very bucked – I can't tell you.

There isn't much news – the weather is dreadful today we had a hail storm.

By the way I've paid your beer-bill to the Grantfield stores – sold the wardrobe to do it & the lino in Grant's room – for housekeeping money. I didn't want to do this – but I couldn't do otherwise.

Will you try & send me as much as you possible can during the next few weeks – I have some pressing accounts that I must pay before I leave. I owe the butcher quite a bit for meat we had when you were here. Since you've been gone I've paid weekly & weeks I could not pay – I didn't have any.

There is also the rent – I had saved up nearly enough – but that went I'm afraid – during the bad period when you were out of work. I do not want to sell the furniture to live on I must have something to come down with.

Have you made arrangement yet about the three tea boxes – I wish to get them out of my way. I have a large number of parcels ready for the post but of course cannot do anything until get some dough. I trust you are not being too optimistic over your job & running up all sorts of debts with Robin Black and others.

When would you like me to come down – if it's convenient to you I would like to get down before the weather breaks & the nights get too dark – of course it is up to you.

Michael is off to the "Fleetie" line tonight – after mackeral [*sic*]. I hope he catches a few.

I haven't answered Mrs Scotts letter yet – so far I've been unsuccessful in getting any wool.

Look after yourself won't you –

Love

Valda

On his 50th birthday, Christopher sustained an injury at work when a bit of hot steel sparked into his right eye. He was also given a week's notice but was almost instantaneously re-employed in "the Stamping Shop, where they make copper belts for shells etc. ... a responsible [job] but physically much lighter work..." In addition, the week previous Christopher had written to his brother severing all relations with him.

Whalsay
19/8/42

My dearest Christopher,

What a dreadful time you've been through, my sweet - & what a miserable birthday you must have had.

I do trust the eye is better & that there will be no after effect – I can't write & tell you just how I felt when I read your letter – the first part – I felt like making straight for Clett Head. What a life! Anyway it's an ill wind that blows etc etc & I'm glad you're into a lighter department. By the way keep your eyes & ears open for a suitable job for me. I'd like to have something to fall into when I come down.

I'm sending on your birthday parcel tomorrow – it's a bit late I'm afraid – but it couldn't be helped – <u>Don't</u> throw the <u>cake</u> <u>tin</u> <u>away</u>. Also sending off orange biscuit tin – just store that as it is.

I've got my sea chest roped up & labelled all ready to send – just waiting for someone to take it up the road.

I haven't answered Mrs Scotts letter yet – have been trying to get hold of some raw wool but it is difficult.

Have been very busy completing an order for Miss Henning but I'll finish it this week – thank Goodness & then be able to rush things forward – but I couldn't afford to let it by – as I'll want a new coat & do not want to come down on you for it.

Very little news here just now. Mike is still getting those sties. By the way how was Orr? Did you have a nice time with him? – you never said.

Excuse this dreadfully dirty paper – but I'm using up all the scraps. I wish you'd go into "digs" you'd be far more comfortable – while the Scotts are away – physically at any rate.

I know how lonely & tired you must be – poor darling – never mind it won't be for much longer. I'll be with you as soon as I can get clear of here – let's hope it will be soon.

All my love dearest

Valda

Wednesday morning

Just going down to post your parcel addressed Christopher Grieve so you'll know it's for you to open not to store.

By now you should have received a Reg. Letter so that will put your mind at ease darling. V.

Sudheim
Whalsay
31/8/42

My dearest Christopher,

I really should have written you on Friday – but felt [?*too*] fagged out – have had a hefty week. Michael has been in bed since a week on Friday (he's up today for the first time) with a really terrifying cold – on Monday he was really ill high fever & gasping for breath – and delirious – fortunately Charles came up - & when he saw how bad he was he went back to his place & came back with pills 3 different kinds of medicine – one kind for the fever – another for his sore throat – one to quieten him & the medicine to loosen his chest – what a time we had – we stayed up with him all night – towards morning he seemed a wee bit easier – so Charles stayed upstairs with him – swathed in one of the striped blankets & reading Joseph Stalin while I snatched an hours sleep on the settee – what a night! I don't want to go through that again. I was scared stiff but fortunately he didn't get worse – it was his breathing that was so terrifying – poor little soul – he never tasted a thing for 3 days except sips of "bland."

I'm OK - & managed to send off one tea box newspapers & one small box on Friday – the orange sea chest went the week before. I've applied for my permit – I hear it takes 3 weeks to get through – but I'm not sure on that point – I hope not because I'll need to get down before the weather breaks.

Thank you for your wire for £4- . I presume you are getting "country money" – are you? I had a form some weeks ago to fill in.

You never answered my question concerning the Faeroese snaps – I told you old Williamson had spoken to me about them – he'd had word from the Danish Consul in Lerwick – I was under the impression you had answered the registered letter I sent to you – you told me you had – but apparently Schache had never heard from you.

In the parcel of books I'm sending on there are "*Green Rushes*" by Walsh - & a copy of *New Writing* which came by the post on Friday.

I hope you have received the cake etc by now - & that the eggs were intact.

Michael is writing you & I see the rubber is much in use – he's looking pretty wan – and thin.

I'm doing you a pair of socks – couldn't get any wool in Lerwick except khaki – I don't suppose you will mind. I knitted Michael a vest last week – hope to do another two before I come down he will then be fitted out for the winter – I expect you need a lot of things.

I'll leave this open until tomorrow – there may be a letter from you. By the way what happened to the Rolls Royce job - ?

Keep your eyes open for a suitable job for me or get some of your friends to do so. I want to get one as soon as we've settled into a place.

Cheerio my darling
All my love

Valda

PS
Hadn't you better write a little note for me to send to Hay & Co. – I'm not like you – I don't like leaving things – it makes a better impression on these kind of people if one faces the music.

Monday

Received your letter today I'm very sorry to hear you've had chill – poor dear.

So you're having to shift from the Scotts is this something new - ? Surely there is no need to take all the parcels with you – especially the ones addressed to me – couldn't they store them until I come down? I'm beginning to wonder where on earth Mike & I will stay when we come down – if ever we get that far. It's a pity in some ways that you quarrelled with Graham – all these things make it so much more difficult.

I'm sorry to keep harping on the money side of things – but do please send me as much as you can – otherwise it will be X'mas before I can leave – the place is desolate & uncomfortable enough now – with every thing gone from it but the bare necessities – and I must keep £20 of the house money to come down with - & I still have quite a few pounds to pay off on the butcher & milk bill – although I put in something every time I get from you & there is also the rent.

I seem to get less from you these day[*s*] than when you were in training – your wage plus your country money can't be less than £4-10-0- to £5. I think you could have managed on £1-10-0 — of course I know it will be more now you're going into digs. It's a pity because it means I'll probably catch the bad weather going down - & I'm bad enough at the best of times. Why didn't you accept the Rolls Royce job? I hope to goodness I get something as soon as I get – even if it only keeps myself. I'm utterly fed up with this uncertainty it's just the devil —

We'll have to away the *Earl* has changed her timetable – she's coming back at dinner time instead of tomorrow for this week.

I hope you've written to me on Sunday as you said – I'm eager to know if you've found suitable digs.

Love

Valda

Give Robin my love – you never mention Margaret B. isn't she in the picture?

Wednesday

[*1942*]

My dear Christopher,

So glad to get your letter today & to know you are improving take it easy old dear - .

I'm sorry to bombard you with boxes but what can I do – Mary could only take three & no one else would be responsible for any more – I haven't sent off any more but will have one with my pots & pans & my trunk but won't send those until the last minute. I think I'll send Mike's bed too instead of selling it – it may come in handy.

We're both down with dreadful chest colds – Charles has gone – so there is no-one now to do things or doctor us – before he went he rounded up Hays - & got me up coal – goodness only knows how I'd have fared if he hadn't – because it['s] been pouring with rain for four days now – & simply impossible to get to the hill – even if I'd been well enough. I'm really worried about Mike – he seems just about played out.

Re letter to Hays – I gather you are sending it from Glasgow – the enclosed was just a copy – make monthly rather than weekly instalments. Will be leaving here either on the Saturday or Tuesday – 3rd or 6th Oct.

Send a little if & when you can – I've paid up the butcher but still have a little on my milk bill.

Longing to see you again

All love

Valda

Christopher then sustained further injuries at work when a pile of copper plates fell on him. He wrote to Valda, "I think I was very lucky. I might easily have had both legs and my left arm fractured, but actually I got off lightly considering the nature of the accident with a badly gashed right leg, a left leg put out of commission altogether with a muscular wrench which has swollen up greatly and which makes it impossible for me to walk, and a whole series of long slashing cuts on my left forearm."

He went to stay with Margaret & Robin Black.

Sudheim

7/9/42

My poor darling,

What rotten luck – I can only hope it is not serious – received the wire on Saturday but had no idea what could be wrong until I received your letter today. Even if it isn't too serious I know how it must have played you up. I only wish we were together again – it seems such years ago since I said goodbye to you on Symbister Pier.

I have one consolation in knowing you are in good hands – please convey my very sincerest thanks to Margaret & Robin. I trust you'll manage to let me have word of you again this week otherwise I'll be terribly worried – thank goodness your legs weren't broken – how on earth did it happen?

Michael is well again – but looking very pale & thin – it is very cold here & of course the house being denuded except for a chair apiece makes it much colder & also looks very cheerless. I only hope I'll be down by the end of the month.

How did you come to be at the Blacks – are the Scotts back yet - ?

Things are going on here much the same as usual. The weather has been dreadful – I'll be sending you a pair of socks next week I expect you'll be in need of them. I'm just finishing the vest for Michael – he'll be set up for underclothes then.

Darling I'm so terribly sorry for you – the Grieves don't seem to have much luck do they? And I do think it is about time we had a spot – but don't worry dearest just hurry up and get fit again.

We'll win through between us somehow –

I sent off a couple more tea boxes last Friday – I'm just about at the end of packing up now – except for Mike's bed & mattress –

My kindest regards to the Blacks & do tell them how grateful I am –

All my love to
yourself darling

Valda

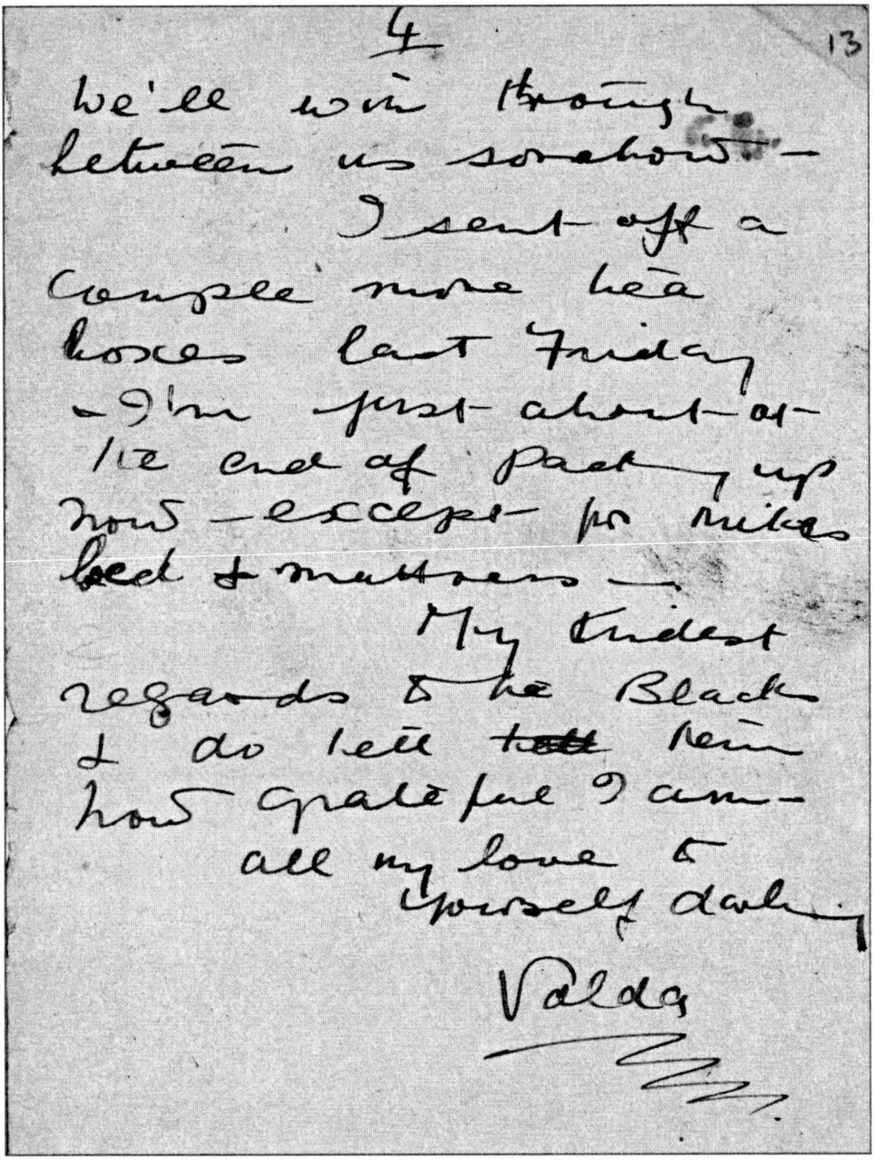
4

13

We'll win through
between us somehow —
I sent off a
couple more tea
boxes last Friday
— I'm just about at
the end of packing up
now — except for Mike's
bed & mattress —.
My kindest
regards to the Black
& do tell ~~tell~~ him
how grateful I am —
all my love to
yourself darling

Valda

Sudheim
Whalsay
11.9.42

My dearest Christopher,

I was so glad to get your letter this morning – no darling I'm not vexed with you I deserve all you said – and a bit more - . Lets forget all about it – we'll soon be together again & then nothing else will matter.[129]

Thank heavens your cuts are healing – and I only hope for your sake your leg will heal up – but as you say these muscular wrenches are the devil. Don't worry about getting back to work too quickly – my only concern about getting money was to enable me to get down before the weather breaks up. I think I'll try & get down providing the weather is fair round about the 29th – will that be OK with you – let me know.

It's been bitterly cold here – yesterday there was sleet – and of course with practically everything out of the house it is pretty cheerless.

I suppose conditions are pretty bad down South.

Yes! I did register some months ago – but have heard nothing since. I'm wondering what sort of job I could get – I'm really not well-equipped as you know – still we'll find something I expect.

It is such a relief to me to know you're in good hands – poor darling – you've never said how it happened – were you working alongside the pillar of plate copper – or piling it up? You must have had a narrow escape.

Will have to finish in pencil – have just [*used*] up all the ink bottle and lost my pen.

[129] All the pressures of wartime on both Christopher and Valda, combined with communicating only by letter for such a lengthy period are beginning to take their toll – readers interested can refer to *NSL*, Christopher's letter of 9 September 1942, pages 240-1.

I'm sending you a pair of socks – the wool is nice & soft – but a horrible colour – but it was the only thing I could get – also a couple of hankies – for which I paid the scandalous price of 1/3 each – but I thought perhaps you would need them. Would you ask Margaret the name of her laundry because I'll pack up the things on the bed when I leave & send them straight to the laundry – that will solve one problem.

I'll say goodnight now dearest –

All my love & get well soon I'm longing to be with you again

Valda

PS
Mike is out again and going to school on Monday – he's very thin & pale.

Sudheim

2/10/42

My dearest Christopher,

I'm leaving here on Tuesday [6] and goodness only knows when we'll reach Glasgow I still seem to have an awful lot of luggage & I'm just wondering how I'll manage – I expect it will be a sore sight.

Mary[130] came in yesterday & washed out the bedrooms, tomorrow she is coming in for the grand finale – I don't know how I'd have managed if it hadn't been for her – she['s] been kindness itself – this week she has given all my meals except my morning cup & damned good meals at that.

I was glad to get your wire & to know you're on the mend – I'm not worrying yet how we'll manage at your end – I've enough worries this end to contend with.

The parcels that I address to 2 Park Terrace[131] are clothes – stuff that I'll need right away.

I'm wiring you tomorrow to put you at ease - & I'm deadly tired tonight can scarcely keep my eyes open – sorry to bum you with the parcels – but what can I do –

Goodnight darling

Valda

130 Mary Williamson, who had also held the 'makkins' of gloves for Valda, along with others. 'After sixty years: once more on the Grieves in Whalsay, 1933-42' by John Manson, in *The New Shetlander* pp. 18, 21.

131 The Blacks.

Valda and (James) Michael left Whalsay on Tuesday 6th October 1942.[132] *Although Valda's letters show she had sent a great deal of Christopher's letters and manuscripts ahead, Michael Grieve nevertheless remembered 'My mother and I sailed in 1942, on the same boat my father had taken, laden with 40 tea-chests crammed with manuscripts and books... The sweetest memories of childhood sank below the horizon and Whalsay, all love, and sorrow, and longing, became a miniaturised complex circuit imprinted on the memory, an electric light to be switched on though fingers fumble at the switch.'*[133]

Michael began at Kilquhanity School[134] *in Kirkcudbrightshire, a progressive boarding school run by John and Morag Aitkenhead.*

In the autumn of 1944, Christopher left the Mechans firm for the Merchant Navy and worked on board a Norwegian ship, the Gurli.[135]

---

[132] Michael's departure is recorded in the Livister school log on 25th September. - Footnote to Brian Smith's essay in *MacDiarmid in Shetland*, ibid.

[133] Michael Grieve in his Foreword to *MacDiarmid in Shetland*, ibid. 'But in reality Valda had sent most of their luggage before they left.' – John Manson, *The New Shetlander* article, ibid, p. 20.

[134] 'It is the only really good experimental school in Scotland .... It is located in lovely country in Wigtonshire and has beautiful grounds, gardens which grow all the necessary vegetables etc. for the school, a dairy which ensures plenty of fresh milk (as well as eggs etc.), a staff of ten teachers of the right sort in addition to the Headmaster, Aitkenhead, himself. And the school is not only run on lines which I feel certain Michael will enjoy immensely but which will be very good indeed for his development, but most of the pupils are about his own age, so that will be nice for him. And Aitkenhead is very keen to have him and will take a personal interest in him...' – Christopher's letter to Valda 21st April 1942, *NSL* p. 225.

[135] See *NSL* pp. 244-5.

27, Arundel Drive
Battlefield
Glasgow S 2
15/3/45

Dear Christopher,

Thank you for your letter – What is done, can't be helped – so the less said about it the better. I know you're not having an easy time - & I'm sorry for you – very sorry – only you make it so difficult for me to give you the help & sympathy I would like to. When you have been drinking – I hate it – and can you blame me – for I know exactly what is going to happen – you are going to say all sorts of nasty things. I am quite prepared to face up to things with you – when you are sober – but not otherwise. I've always been fond of you & have always done my best for you - under trying circumstances for a young girl – now I am older I just can't "take it" – that is all. I think that is easily explainable & reasonable.

My lack of interest is untrue – it is true that I cannot agree with you on all subjects I do on the main ones – so I do not see you have anything to grumble about.

I'm going down to see Bill[136] today as so far nothing has arrived from him or from Dakers[137].

Mike won't be home for another fortnight at the least - & will be home for a month so you will have plenty of chance of seeing him.

Now cheer up & pull yourself together.

Love
Valda

---

136 Probably William MacLellan, Glasgow publisher of some of MacDiarmid's work, incl. *Selected Poems* (1944); later publications incl. *A Kist of Whistles: New Poems* (1947), *In Memoriam James Joyce* (1955) and numerous books to which MacDiarmid had contributed, e.g. *Scottish Art and Letters* (1946), *Poetry Scotland: Third Collection* (1946). MacLellan also published Edwin Morgan's first book, *The Vision of Cathkin Braes*, in 1952.

137 Publisher Andrew Dakers Ltd. (London). MacDiarmid was editing and writing an introductory essay for William Soutar's *Collected Poems,* which would be published by Dakers in 1948. On 23rd January he'd written from the *Gurli* to Helen Cruickshank, 'I am due – ovedue 10 days' leave: but can't get it until we are running again. Which is a nuisance. As I can't finish my work on Soutar's *Collected Poems* till then. That task has been worrying me for a long time. It proved very much harder than I had anticipated – owing to the great mass of material...' (*NSL*, p. 246).

Sunday

[*1945*]

Dear Christopher,

Whats happened to you – I was expecting you home last night & had the tea waiting for you. I'm enclosing this note in with Anders[138] instead of enclosing Anders in with yours as I should do in case you come home before this reaches Rothesay (I've no idea how the mail is there) and I want Olsen to get my note – as there is a Picture I would like to see "*A Cornish Rhapsody*."[139]

I am wondering if the reason you did not come home was because I did not send you any money I was going to – but it would run me <u>very</u> short and Anders said you could ask him for it – after all there was a lot to do with the money this pay day – Mike going away – the electric Bill to pay etc –

You may be sure I haven't blown it in – the extent to which I have spent on myself amounts to 5/3 – so what!

There are a few letters here for you – one from Dakers & one from Maurice Lindsay – Douglas Young's[140] father is dead. The calendars will be ready definitely this weekend, Robin is bringing them out.[141] Letter from America "trusting your MSS. hasn't gone in the deep sea["] & that is all. I'm glad you did not come home at the beginning of the week for my boiler burst & I had to have the whole range taken out & no fire for 3 days.

All the best

Love

Valda

---

[138] Anders Olsen was the skipper of the *Gurli* at this time.

[139] '*The Cornish Rhapsody*' composed by Hubert Bath (1883-1945) was in fact the score to the 1944 film called *Love Story* (no relation to the 1970 film of same name), starring Margaret Lockwood & Stewart Granger.

[140] Scots poet, translator into Scots (incl. Lord's my herd, 1943, the 23rd psalm in Scots verse), polymath. (*cf.* recent Scots version 23rd psalm by Diana Hendry.)

[141] Robin Black published Scots Makars Calendars for 1945 with a MacDiarmid poem for every month of the year.

The editor of the Carlisle Journal *invited Hugh MacDiarmid to work for the paper, a position he took up in May 1947, covering all and sundry events, 'City Council meetings, Divorce Courts, Cinemas, Theatre, Football and Boxing Matches etc. etc.'.*[142]

Valda appears to have made a visit to Cornwall, whilst Michael is in his residential school.

1947 [*4 July*]
POSTCARD
From Bude Cornwall

Christopher Grieve
C/o The Carlisle Journal
60, English Street
Carlisle
England

Friday
No word from you yet – will you let me have the address of Charles Lahr per return (shop address) I may have a few hours to spare on Wednesday.

Love Valda

[142] *NSL*, p. 249.

32, Victoria Crescent Road
Wednesday
[*Wed. 16 July 1947*]

My dear Christopher,

Many thanks for your wire & letters – I will take your card down to the Insurance people this week without fail.

I do not think you read my letters – it was Thursday morning – I was in Carlisle about 8 am – it was a 16 hours journey by the 'bus and I was a bit done in – as I had been travelling since 9 am the Wednesday morning and did not reach Glasgow until 12 o'clock mid-day on Thursday.

Now I want you to read what I'm going to say now carefully – because there will be no excuse for you to say you did not know anything about it.

The first is this – Michael is due home tomorrow Thursday July 17th and from now on – I expect money from you weekly – Michael must have fairly decent meals each day – even if you do not think it necessary for me to have them. Now that your Income Tax is reduced – you have far less excuse for your neglect. I noted what you said about one week – that a bet you made – did [*sic*] come off – I'm sorry it didn't – but I'm also aware that a 7/6 bet did not really make any difference to my weeks allowance – I think it is high time you gave me a little credit for some intelligence – it is rather wearisome to be always treated as a very small child or someone mentally deficient.

I am serious about this - . I made some threats a few weeks ago – by now you have probably forgotten – one was that if you did not send me an allowance each week – that I would (1) apply for Parish Relief (2) Interview the directors of *Carlisle Journal* (3) Take a job & bust the whole thing up.[143]

[143] On the Friday [*very likely 18th July 1947*] Christopher replied, 'The very last thing in the world I want is to break with you. You must know that perfectly well. Any such break would finish me completely. I have explained the horrible way things have turned out here financially - ...' – *NSL*, p. 248.

Quite frankly I do not want to do any of these things – but this is a threat no longer – it is a promise.

While Michael is at home I must have means to support him regularly. You've had plenty of extra money these past few weeks – and I haven't seen any of it – and there is still £5 owing John Aitkenhead – but I don't suppose that worries you – well it does me.

I had to borrow from my aunts money to pay for the extras on my journey back – meals – taxi's etc. I sent her a £1 (it was £2 I borrowed) on receiving your wire. I owe Sadie for 4 bag of coal she got while I was away – and that reminds me – I told you a couple of weeks before my holidays that I am due out [*of*] here the second week in Aug. – Sadies (poor woman has to get out of her place and she[*'s*] coming here – I've heard you talk of "your pride" before – well perhaps you can think of mine – it's not very nice living on here & not being able to pay rent.

I noted what you said about the portable wireless for my birthday – I thank you very much, Christopher for the nice thought —

I feel very much the better for my holiday – and I realised very much – when I was at home – how much I'll miss them when I go – for it will mean I will have no-one to lean on consciously and unconsciously when they are dead – it's rather an awful thought.

Also I do not know what you're doing about your laundry – it must be filthy by now – it's not fair asking me to wash such dirty stuff – as it must be by now – if you have not had it washed in the interval – don't you realise Christopher that even if you can't smell yourself – other people can. You have paper & string so there is no excuse – and what with coupons etc to wear your new socks until they fall off you –

By now you will have got your new ration book. Will you please cut out the <u>coupon book</u> & send it on to me – otherwise you will be losing it – or giving your coupons away & we can't afford to have that happen – poor Michael has grown out of all his Jackets & his Mac – he was feeling a bit sore about it the last time he was at home – that he never got any new clothes – he's just at the age to become a bit clothes conscious – and apart from that – he really needs them.

I've started packing up some of my own books – you'd better let me know what you want done with yours – it is impossible to leave it all until the last minute.

With love
Valda

PTO
I liked the Photo of your head by Benno[144] – he showed it to me before he sent it on to you –

Valda

[144] Benno Schotz, sculptor.

32 Victoria Crescent Road
Glasgow W2
[?22 *July 1947*]

Tuesday

My dear Christopher,

Thank you very much for the wire received on Friday – I was down to 3D so you can guess how well pleased I was to get it.

I think Michael is looking a bit pale – he is probably growing too fast.

I received your very small parcel of laundry – yesterday I washed but could not dry it – because of the pelting rain – but I'll get it ironed and away by Thursday and in a box which you can keep and send back again with laundry – by the way I think you could have sent more pairs of socks and also what has happened to your striped shirts – you've never said whether you like the navy shirt I sent you — ?

Are you going to the Langholm Common Riding ? And did you go to Ireland?

I meant to have written you on Sunday – but Hamish Henderson turned up unexpectedly on Saturday – I took him out to Scotts on Sunday and we had a good time – F.G. was in a good mood and sang a number of songs. Hamish is going to call on you on his way down. He goes to Germany on the 31st of this month.

I've heard rumours that MacLennan [*MacLellan*] is getting you to defend him in his conduct over the Dunedin Society – now don't let Bill put any pressure on you because you owe him a few pounds – it's not worth it.

And I've kept the nice thing for last – your broadcast last night was splendid in every way. It was definitely your best – you spoke very clear and unhurried and for the first time for a long time I felt proud of you.

With love
Valda xxx

PS
Michael is having a somewhat amusing if not boring time – teaching me to ride my bicycle up & down Great Western Road to get use to traffic and of course I disgrace myself every time by falling off once or twice during the evening — V.

Glasgow W2

[*last week July 1947*]

My dear Christopher,

Thank you for ringing me up and letting me know the reason for your not writing – and also for your long letter of explanation – I'm afraid it reminded me of one of Churchill's war speeches.

I quite understand all your difficulties – and in some ways I'm sorry for you – but not enough to become soft or unintelligent over them. I quite appreciate that having arrived back so late you could not send the wire that evening – but surely you could have sent it the next day – also that if you can afford to spend 3 days in Liverpool waiting for a plane (with the money to pay for your plane) you could also have sent me something. I have no idea how you expect me to live – on air – or on the charity of your friends? It was very lucky for you that you sent the P.O. for 12/6 – for 3 days we did not have any butter or marg in the house – as I had not the wherewithal for the rations. I presume you are not going without your smokes – or your beer – or a certain amount of food per day – well more often than not I have to go without smokes – and with only a bare amount of food. It's not good enough on £7-10- per week- and Christopher I'm not making any more sacrifices for you.

As for your work – well it's hard for me to say anything about it – but I think if you really wanted to do something you'd manage it somehow – now your excuse is you have no time. No this – no that – when you were here it was just the same. You had the time but you preferred other things – now you're working 14-15-hours per day – so they just cancel each other out.

Michael was disappointed you did not send him anything for his birthday – it's never the same to a kid getting it afterwards.

By the way he does not want an expensive tailored suit – all he wants at the moment is a pair of long slacks & a sports jacket so that when he visits the other boys' houses he doesn't look like something from the slums – it's not fair at his age that he should have to go about like that. It's no use saying you're doing your best – that's a lie – and you've always been good at lying. If you felt any sense of responsibility towards Michael or myself knowing how weak you are with money – you would have seen that some of the cheque[*s*] at least from your various BBC contracts & articles were sent on to me. But you are completely unscrupulous in this matter.

I've written to Mrs Downie and I'm hoping to go to her next week – if I cannot find a place then I will have to try & make some arrangements with the *Carlisle Journal* that £2 at least of your salary is sent to me. I'm not asking for much – just enough for the bare necessities & to keep a roof over my head.

I've been patient long enough – too long in fact – and I'm not now prepared to accept any excuses – anyway I have to be out of here this next month – and have enough to worry about with[*out*] your adding to them.

Please remember that Michael cannot go back to school next term unless £5 is paid up that I owe John.

I'm glad you enjoyed the Langholm Common Riding[145] – it must have been most impressive.

The weather here is quite good for the last two days. Yesterday Aline Galloway and I cycled to Milngavie. We only took 35 minutes. I am now getting quite good at cycling.

Re your laundry – you can quite easily send your laundry once a fortnight for the next few weeks that I'm here – I'm certainly not going to wash anything again that has been worn for weeks on end – you could not ask a laundry to do it so why ask your wife. That's different, of course – well it isn't from now on.

145 Held last Friday in July – 25th in 1947 – to protect the boundaries of the land belonging to the community.

I was at F.G.'s the other night – he's much brighter than he'd been for a long time.

Well I must stop and get this posted as I'd like it to reach you before the weekend -

With every good wish

Valda

Kilquhanity
Sunday

Dear Christopher –

This is to let you know I arrived safely after having to change buses six times – Michael met me at Dumfries – so we had tea there & then got a bus to Springholm – walked to Kirkpatrick Durham & then being in a lavish mood – we took a car to Kilquhanity – had a nice evening – gathering in the hay & then had supper with John & Morag – getting to bed at 1.30 AM

Today has been lovely – did a big wash & ironing – sunbathed – listened to a musical concert – went a walk & I'm now writing this in John Wood[*s*] place – we're going to have a bean feast this evening – Michael is looking well – we had some lovely home-baked bread today which he had made

Irma & Ian Woods are grand people in a very real sense – it is a pity that there aren't more such people – at this kind of school – I feel that John is not in good form & that compared to Ian he is very immature - & resenting his maturity. Now do look after yourself - & see that you get enough to eat – ask Mrs Gibson for anything you want. Give Lisa a pat - & my regards to Mrs Gibson –

Love to yourself

Valda xxx

Part 3

Brownsbank and Beyond

In January 1951, the Grieves moved to Brownsbank Cottage, Lanarkshire. Valda returned to Cornwall periodically, when her family there needed her. Christopher continued to travel widely in this period (he had visited the Soviet Union in October-November 1950 where he met most of the leading Russian writers, and in the summer of 1951 had been guest of honour at the World Youth Festival in East Berlin, broadcast about this from Radio Budapest & Radio Prague, met Pablo Neruda, Nazim Hikmet & others[146]*), his exact whereabouts not always being known to Valda, again something she seems to have taken entirely in her stride.*

Thursday morning
28, King Street
Bude
Nth Cornwall

[?*September 1953*]

My dearest Christopher & Michael (if you're there),

Sorry that I haven't managed a letter before – it's practically impossible to write, read or knit – not that I'm doing anything in particular except wash dishes – my God – you think you've a lot of dishes to wash from one meal to the other – you should see here – the first morning I was home Aunt Jane was all dithery – I had 8 cups (for 3 people) six or seven knives – beside the necessary things –

The whole set up is fantastic – and pathetic – like a scene from a satire play.

Thank you for your two letters – that & the fact that I arrived home "decently" clad has redeemed you in my aunts' eyes.

[146] Christopher's letter to Miss Edith Trelease Aney at the University of Philadelphia, *NSL*, pp. 287-91.

Aunt Agnes is very ill no hope of recovery so the Dr told me – her kidneys are now giving out but neither she or Aunt Jane know this so don't say anything about it in any subsequent letters.

I had a lovely time in London as Mike will tell you – I enjoyed it so much that I did not want to stay another day. [*sic*]

Breaking the journey made it much nicer – home here I'm going to bed at 9 pm – dead beat. Aunt Jane is <u>very</u> deaf & I have to shout the whole time – also there is so much noise in the house banging of dishes & buckets – she doesn't hear it, you see.

Bude has altered very much for the worse. The camp at Cleave (3,000) having spoilt it – snack bars all over the place.

I'm very much struck with the quality of light here – it's the same intense whiteness like you get in Scotland – England was quite different.

I've met a lot of people I know - & hearing the most awful tales of myself –

"You'rn was a mighty purty little maid."

"You'rn was a brave little maid."

"You'rn was supernatural you'rn was afraid of nothing."

"Do you remember the time you fell in the canal & swam across with your leather coat & wellingtons on – you'rn was so heavy we had to pull you out."

"What about the time you fell over Compass Point – you didn't loose you're head but you was frighten & came running to me afterwards – I was picking blackberry at the bottom of the cliff & saw you fall."

And so on & so on.

- I look a lot younger than most all of the people my own age & some younger.

I'm glad dear you are managing to have a bit of fun etc – I feel quite envious.

Hope Mr Todd brings you a pie.

Has Mike arrived back yet – hope he had a good journey up – he was certainly lucky going down.

Give Nan & Bill[147] my salutations. Hope you're getting enough to eat – we're having roast duck & sage & onion stuffing on Sunday.

Went out & bought a portable wireless for my aunts (they paid) this week – a super one – in red leather – a Roberts make £20 – a little smaller than ours & much nicer looking – hope they'll get some use from it.

Will you ask Mike the next time he's going into Biggar to post on my brown swagger coat – not the Harris tweed – the one that's over your kilt jacket – just roll it up anyhow in a parcel – it may fit one of my aunts & would save them buying.

The clatter of dinner has started – sorry this isn't an interesting letter – but it is quite impossible to think.

So cheerio for now – remind me to Mrs Jackson[148] when you see her. I sent P.C.'s from London but have a feeling I did[*n't*] address them sufficiently.

All my love to you both

Valda X

[147] William MacLellan, publisher (as above, p. 152) and Agnes (Nan) Walker, his wife.

[148] Mrs Jackson was a neighbour at Candymill, who used to help out Christopher & Valda in the house. She 'became a good friend and frequent reliable overseer of their domestic arrangements.'(Deirdre Grieve, corresp.).

<u>Sunday</u> [*September 1953*]
28, King Street
Bude
Nth Cornwall

My dearest Christopher & Michael,

Well, Sunday is nearly over - & I'm thankful – the aunts are so difficult that I'm "wappit" out doing nothing but having to listen to them. I had a good cry today – it is so pathetic yet so nerve wrecking & horrible in a way – don't make any mention of the things I say in my letter as they read everything when my back is turned.

We had roast duck & stuffing, roast potatoes & peas today for dinner – I'd rather have had boiled beans than all the fuss they made of cooking it – snarling at each other – grunting – talking to themselves it's like living in a madhouse in some ways – at other times everything is normal & then this breaks out again.

By the way do not bother to send on the coat mentioned in last letter as they've decided to get a new one. The wireless they've got is super duper as Mike would say – a Roberts portable in red leatherette – known as the Rolls Royce of portable – cost £20.7.6.

Today has been the first glorious day – the sun a scorcher - & what a sunset tonight – flame-orange & red shading into dove grey sea.

I'm sending on a couple of saffron cakes tomorrow - & maybe a pasty.

Hope you're managing to see a bit of the Festival.

I note what you say about R.D. Smith & the [??*Drunk Man*] – have you heard anything definite about the Bruce programme?

By the way what['*s*] happen[*ing*] about the GreyWalls Press – perhaps I could call & see the lawyer if nothing satisfactory has happen[*ed*] – let me know.

I've booked a trip for [?*Fowey*] & [?*Mevagissey*][149] Can't spell it – for Thursday – must get somewhere before the holiday is over.

---

149 A summer passenger ferry runs from Fowey to Mevagissey.

There's a sheet out in the shed – perhaps you'll send it to the laundry Mike – he comes on Wednesday afternoons about 2.30 pm. Mrs Jackson will take it in for you – I had a nice letter from her.

Do hope you're managing to feed yourselves alright – when the first lot of peas are done don't forget to pull up the roots & put them in [?] – they make good manure. I was glad to hear Mike got back safely – without too much difficulty.

Will get this posted tonight & it will then go out first thing tomorrow morning.

Do look after yourselves. Thanks for your letter Mike - & don't pass rude remarks over my writing – it's this hellish Biro – it just runs away with you

All my love my two dears
Yours
Valda X

PS Did I tell you that I had a talk with the Dr & my aunt can't recover it's only a matter of time – her kidneys are now giving out but I have not told the other aunt this – goodness only knows what is going to happen.

Wednesday

Dear Christopher & Mike,

Do hope these pasties arrive in fairly good condition – had another scorcher yesterday but today is dull & I think going to be wet. Hope you're making good use of the peas & beans – they are over down here – give Janey[150] any bits a piece of pasty from me – Judy I know will be looked after & if not make herself heard – but my gentle self-effacing Bitsie is different –

all my love to you Christopher & Mike

Valda X

[150] Border Terrier. Judy was likely to have been the cat.

Sunday
28 King Street
Bude
Nth Cornwall

My dearest Christopher,

'Fraid I haven't done much reading – find it quite impossible to think at all – it's like being shut up.

We've spent the whole day cooking & washing up – a wonderful meal – but what a lot of work. Had a nice letter from Isabel.[151] How have you enjoyed the Festival – did you get any tickets from Bill? This is my last week – will be starting for home next Tuesday I think – 22nd. Tell Mike if you're hungry to make a parsley tart – short crust – line sandwich tin – put plenty of roughly chopped parsley – a couple of eggs beaten with little milk – salt & pepper & top crust.

Hope you've managed O.K. for money – and I trust the cakes & pasties arrived in good condition. I'm going to Looe & Polperro on Tuesday. Have just had two days away. Sorry my letters are so inadequate but I'm terribly tired – not because I've been doing a lot – think it's the restlessness of the house. My love Christopher,

Valda   Love to you Mike

[151] Isabel MacCaig, wife of poet Norman MacCaig.

[? *1953*]
28, King Street
Bude
Nth Cornwall

My dearest Christopher,

Many thanks for your letter and the £2. I was very glad of it – for altho' I haven't done anything money seems to slip away unseen. I do hope you & Mike have managed OK & not been too short.

I sent Nan a wire to the BBC yesterday & listened in to her concert[152] from a neighbour's house as the set here is only a portable & not strong enough to get the Scottish station – thought it very good indeed. Wasn't very impressed with Ewan's[153] ballads on the Third programme – there's a sameness about them all. Have you heard anything re. *The Drunk Man*?[154] I thought I was going to get started from here on Tuesday but doubt it – I'll get everything packed for Tuesday ready to go but will probably stay until Thursday – to ease the situation – poor little Aunt Jane is crying in corners – because things are getting too much for her – a couple of days ago she was pouring boiling water from the kettle into a jug & poured it over her hand instead – today she capsized the new-made pot of tea over herself. Another day she nearly knocked herself out by ramming her head against the lavatory door – apart from the two days I had for the motor tours I haven't been anywhere not even to the breakwater so don't get ideas into your head that I've been having a gay old time of it.

How is Michael's cold – do hope it did not come to a really bad one – tell him I'll be home as soon as I can now – I sent on one parcel yesterday there is no need to open it as it only contains some clothes – the same applys [*sic*] to another one (large) which I will send on

152 Agnes (Nan) Walker, William MacLellan's wife, was a pianist.

153 Ewan MacColl (1915-1989), songwriter, folk singer, poet, playwright, activist. Files released at the UK's National Archives in March 2006 show MacColl had been closely monitored by MI5; MacColl and his first wife, Joan Littlewood, were under surveillance during the Second World War, when they lived in Hyde, Cheshire. (*Guardian*, 6.03.06).

154 There had been plans afoot to do something re. *A Drunk Man Looks at the Thistle* at an Edinburgh Festival (?Edinburgh People's Festival) (*NSL*, pp. 303, 301).

at the beginning of the week – a small one marked flowers will you open – just dig a pit somewhere in the veg. garden & put the roots in altogether that will keep them fresh until I get back.

If you want me to call on that lawyer you'd better send me his address.

Do hope dear you're keeping fit – and behaving yourself. I admire your fortitude in going to the farm – it just shows you.

Tell Mike not to be too disappointed if he does not pass his Exam – tell him I'll write him this weekend.

My aunts send you their kindest regards I'm sure they think you're a reformed character & I have not disillusioned them now – no rude remarks – I guess I'll be glad to be back – but I don't think it will be long before I'll have to go again. Aunt Agnes is only hanging on by a thread – and I don't [*know*] what is to happen to Aunt Jane. I'm worried stiff – it seems such a pity that they couldn't have ended their days peaceably. She's [?*worn*] to a shadow.

Sorry I've been so long Christopher – but will be back very soon now – will wire you from London

All my love

Valda X

POSTCARD from London 28 Sept 1953

To C.M. Grieve Esq
Brownsbank Cottage
Biggar
Lanarkshire Scotland

4pm Monday
Just arrived Waterloo – going to look for Leland[155] – lovely weather – Love Valda X

[155] Leland was the Christian name of the wife of Tony Cronin, the poet (Deirdre Grieve, correspondence). Anthony Cronin is anthologised in several collections, incl. *The Faber Book of*

Thursday [3 *June 1954*]

Everything under control – funeral[156] today – Aunt Jane wonderful. We woke up at 6.30 am this morning. Everything redd up by 10 am poor old soul is very upset but keeping the flag flying.

Will write you at weekend – the journey wasn't bad at all. Do hope Mike is feeling very much better – look after yourself Christopher dear - All my love

Valda X

Twentieth Century Verse, edited by John Heath-Stubbs and David Wright (London: Faber, 1967).

156 Valda's Aunt Agnes died on Saturday, 29th May, 1954. By my reckoning, she would have been aged 72 years.

[5 *June* 1954]
Saturday
28, King Street
Bude

My dearest Christopher & Mike,

This is just a short note – must get this posted before 1 pm then you'll get it on Monday morning.

I'm sorry to hear about Mike – be sure he gets proper attention – you can always get Mrs Tweedie[157] to phone Dr Marshall from the farm.

Aunt Jane is being very difficult she hasn't broken down but is on the go all the time – we're up at 6 am each morning & walk – she traipses me all over the place but do not mention anything about "doing too much" in your letter – in case she gets hold of them – I'd never hear the last of it. The funeral went off alright & the tea party afterwards with 4 old ladies – full of a Methodist preacher who had been found in a car with a man – with just her nightdress on & her throat slashed – turned into a vicious & tawdry affair – which I thought very funny – must try to remember & tell you – forgive this short note but Aunt Jane doesn't like to see me sitting down reading or writin' –

Take care of yourselves & behave yourselves – tell Mike he's not to go back to work until he's fit. You'd better put the cat & kitten out in the shed at night – did not think to tell you before. Enclosing £1 Christopher as promised all my love to the two of you.

Valda X

Ask Mrs Jackson for potatoes.

---

157 The Tweedies owned the farm of which Brownsbank Cottage was a part. William MacLellan introduced the Grieves to the Tweedies, who let the Grieves stay in Brownsbank rent-free.

28, King Street
Bude
Nth Cornwall

Thursday

Dearest Christopher,

I missed the mid-day post today so I don't think you will get this until Sat. possible Monday – trust you won't be worried – I was very glad to get your letter – was wondering why you had not written for just over the week but put it down to your overstaying in Edinburgh. I do hope you've been looking after yourself.

I'm leaving here on Sat. morning – had a letter from Barbara[158] she is looking forward to seeing me & we've been invited to Rappaports[159] for Sunday evening. I'll be home on Tuesday –Wednesday at the latest – do trust you'll be home with a good fire burning & a cup of tea – it just depends what happens on Monday.

Hope you're looking forward to seeing me back again – for I shall be glad to see you.

I'm not at all happy at leaving my aunt this time – but what can one do –

all news darling when we meet –

Love
Valda

Enclosing £1.

[158] Barbara Niven, still a close friend (see above, p. 44).

[159] Friends of the Grieves in London. Rappaport was a Communist doctor of medicine.

Sunday 27th

[*June 1954*]

28, King Street

Bude

Nth Cornwall

My dearest Christopher,

Probably this is the first time I've really appreciated you and your many good points – I don't know when I've so looked forward to seeing your face.

Aunt Jane has nearly driven me mazed.

I'll be leaving here on Thursday instead of Wednesday because otherwise I won't be able to see Barbara – and collect your books. I'll be catching the 10 something train on Friday morning from London - & should be at Brownsbank by the 7.15 pm passing Candymill so have a nice cup of tea ready for me – that's a darling.

Sorry I'll be a day later than I originally intended, but I'd like to see Barbara. Hang on to your pension - my sweet - one day later in cashing it won't hurt. So you're still thinking of going to Ireland – think I'd rather have a damn good rest at Brownsbank – but we'll hear all the news when we meet. Will send you the usual saffron cake midweek – and Penguin.

Read the enclosed – what the stars say. Wish I was home – darling.

Love

Valda X

Did you see about the GreyWalls Press? Right as usual!

POSTCARD

Brodick Isle of Arran

28 Aug. '54

Friday

Have been out in a boat fishing – caught 2 fish but had to come in – feeling sea sick. Quite nice weather –

Love

Valda

Brownsbank Cottage
Candymill
by Biggar

5/7/55

Dearest Christopher,

Very glad to get your P.C.'s[160] and the wire – that was more than I expected. It's nice to know you are enjoying yourself & that you found some friends there – hope you got Tom Murray's letter with Jessie Scott's[161] address.

Nothing much doing here – have had a very quiet time – went to the Highland Show, held in Edinburgh this time, with the Tweedies & Mrs Jackson – also had a few hours in Edinburgh when I went about my teeth – but came home on the 6.15pm bus. Had a very quiet birthday – Mrs J & I drank a bottle of cider & that was all. Mike turned up on Sat. late with a lovely bunch of pink carnations & yellow roses & a bottle of Miss Dior perfume – so maybe I don't feel so old after all. If you travel up overnight & the train gets in in time – 6.30 a.m isn't it - & you feel you'd like to come straight through – there is a bus leaving Queen St. (or catch it opposite side entrance

[160] Valda is likely referring to cards from Christopher's trip to Czechoslovakia.

[161] Jessie Scott was an Edinburgh woman who married a Czech airman and became Kotmanova. She was a good friend and a lecturer at Brno University in Czechoslovakia.

Cally Station [)] at 7 am – it would probably be quicker to take a taxi to the West End & get it there – that gives you another 6 – 7 minutes.

We've had dreadful weather – last week it rained solidly for 3 days. Hope the watch kept good time & did not let you down or you it. No reviews of the *Joyce*[162] yet – BBC are wetting their breeks wondering who they can get to review it for Scottish Arts & Letters. *Lines* are the same – wild suggestions going around – Auden – Ezra Pound - & some other bugger I've forgotten the name – not Louis McNiece[163] – but someone like him. Think you went to see him once when we were in London (at Cambridge)

Looking forward to seeing you again Christopher
All my love
Valda

Love to all at Parkhill. Thank B. for her letter.

[162] It was in this year William MacLellan (Glasgow) published MacDiarmid's *In Memoriam James Joyce*.

[163] The poet Louis MacNeice (1907-1963) also worked as a writer and producer for BBC radio. *Lines Review* (No. 9, Aug. 1955) published a review of IMJJ by David Daiches (1912-2005). As for the BBC's quandary, '*A Contemporary Review of IMJJ*' by J.F. Hendry (1912-1986) was broadcast by BBC radio in 1955 and is published by *Chapman* (MacDiarmid Centenary Issue, No. 69-70, Summer/Autumn 1992, p. 158).

[*1955*]
28, King Street
Bude
Nth Cornwall

Oct. 8th

My dearest Christopher,

This is rather later than I meant – but I've never had a chance to get down to writing – my poor old aunt talks so much.

Things here aren't too bad – but I think she finds it very lonely – she's had the place newly decorated & it's looking lovely – but I think the neighbours are a bit jealous. You know how it is – they are not prepared to spend the time or the money on their place – like my aunt does.

Today is lovely – but Wed. Thurs. & Friday it rained all the time – the first rain they've had here for 5 months.

Before I forget you should write to Crawford – Thomson – my fellow sleeper going down to London is a great friend of his and he's been pretty bad with the 'flu (Miss Margaret Gibbons)

Do hope you are managing OK & that Michael managed to come for the weekend.

I'll write him tomorrow.

Have you done your lecture? be careful darling coming back from Edinburgh.

Do you know there really isn't a scrap of news that would be of interest to you – will probably think of things once I get settled in.

Take care of yourself & give my love to Mike —

all my love
Valda x

[1955]
28, King Street
Bude
Nth Cornwall

Tuesday morning

Dear Christopher,

I'm enclosing £1- as promised – have nearly completed your National Health Stamps – had to get nearly £6 worth & will send it to you next week – you've to send it on to Lanark, after signing.

I keep wondering how you are managing – I do hope you are looking after yourself in the right way. I worry quite a bit about you between all my other worries – are you getting enough to eat? Glad you had a nice time at Alloa - & that the Rotary address went down well. Had a short letter from Mike[164] – I told him he should get a Dr in Alloa & get a tonic.

The weather here is very bad. Tomorrow I'm sending on 2 more saffron cakes. Did the others arrive in good condition – or not?

I'm writing to Barbara this week to ask her if I can spend a night with her at the end of the month. I'm waiting on to get Aunt Agnes money settled – it's only a few hundreds – but poor Aunt Jane is really upset with all the bother the lawyers are making – signing this & that – she's quite bewildered & indignant.

I'm not a good letter writer at any time – but having to write mid-morning is paralysing – for that is the only chance I get. Must post this by 1 pm then you should get it tomorrow – hope you're getting some meat from the butcher. Mrs Jackson would cook it for you if you asked her.

[164] Then a reporter on the Alloa Journal (Deirdre Grieve, corresp.)

I'll be glad to get home again – three to four weeks is too long to be away –

All my love darling
Valda X

Will send Howard Fast's[165] book & one on Cornwall in parcel – also bought today Cheyneys "You can't hit a Lady."[166]

[165] Howard Melvin Fast (1914-2003), prolific American author; he refused to cooperate with the House un-American activities committee and as a result served 3 months in prison. Received Stalin peace prize in 1954, two years before Khrushchev's speech on Stalin's crimes, after which three quarters of US Communists left the Party.

[166] Probably Peter Cheyney's (1896-1951) *You Can't Hit a Woman and Other Stories* (1937).

28, King Street
Bude
Nth Cornwall

Wed. 12th

My dearest Christopher,

Many thank[*s*] for your short note etc. — .

We are having wonderful weather – except for the first two days – I haven't worn a coat & left off all I could underneath.

I sincerely hope the lecture went off – O.K. - & that you've arrived back at the cottage. By the way – I think I've mentioned this before – I dislike intensely being address[*ed*] as "my dearest V" – I hate it & loathe it — it makes me howl with rage – so if you cannot write my name Id rather you did not start the letter in the normal conventional way – but just get on with what you're going to say.

Thank you for send[*ing*] on letters – I meant to have told you but forgot – when I was in on Tuesday – the girl behind the [*counter*] suggested it – we were talking - & I said I was going away for a month – so she said would you like us to forward them – I thought it was a good idea especially if Jessie started anticing [*sic*] up each week - & so relieve you of any Temptation – the morning after the night before. "The best laid plans of mice & men gang – " [*added in corner*: is it "agley" ?] – forgotten the ending – I'm enclosing £1- as promised do hope you are managing O.K with cooking etc. - & then the parcel I sent yesterday should arrive on Thursday. I don't think it matters much re. the *Drunk man* – it's only 2 weeks before I'll be home & there are some who have been waiting a long time I'd like to get those done – also if you did them it would parcelling them up & getting to Biggar with them – it's been so long now that another couple of weeks won't make much difference. What do you think?

Met a man here – when we went to see about the gravestone – his son-in-law is a professor at Aberdeen University.

That's about all the news – do hope I'll get a letter from you to hear how things are going.

Isn't it lovely to have the peace & quietness you are always hankering after – I trust you make the best use of it.

All my love – my dear Christopher —

Your obedient wife

Valda X

PS Letter from America was from Robert Carron

Wednesday

28, King Street
Bude
Nth Cornwall

Dear Christopher,

Just going up to post these saffron cakes – you should get them by Friday – had letter from Michael today he says the weather is very bad – and that both of you have had colds – mine never got any worse – and have only a snuffle left. Glad you had a nice time on Saturday with Norman & Crombie[167] – hear you're going to Edinburgh this weekend for the Miners concert – that will make a break.

Today the weather is lovely – brilliant sunshine – and not at all cold. Everyone down here has their windows open – in almost any weather.

Yesterday I bought a really nice pewter teapot – tall and embossed with a spray of flowers on the handle – for 5/- it leaks but have been soldering it & now it's O.K. – looks lovely with flowers in it — also bought a pewter mug in good condition.

There isn't any news here – of course my aunt is much better than I expected & we're keeping better hours so life is easy. She's upstairs cleaning the windows just now as if her life depended on it.

Hope you're taking care of yourself do be careful with the lamp. Will write again at the end of the week –

All love

Valda X

[167] Poets Norman MacCaig (1910-1996) & Crombie Saunders (1914-1991). Crombie Saunders had edited *Selected Poems of Hugh MacDiarmid* (Glasgow: MacLellan, 1944).

28 King Street
Bude

Friday morning

Dear Christopher –

Another lovely day just like Spring – have been out shopping without a coat – it's really a treat.

Days are flying past & it won't be long until I'm home again — take care of your dear self & I do hope your cold is better – be sure to keep bottles in the bed.

Aunt Jane & I are under the weather today – yesterday for tea we ate far too much turnip pasty & cream. I'm feeling the effect of it & I don't know how bad she is – but she's belching all over the place in a genteel way & won't own up to over-eating.

I hope you have a good time at the Miners concert.

Here is another thriller – will see what's in the shops today – maybe I'll pick up another.

Give my regards to Mrs Jackson when you see her. Hope you are managing O.K. – now don't forget to ask if you need anything.

Hope to get another walk today – if all goes well – and she does not want to go to the church yard.

Will write again at the beginning of the week.

All my love

Valda X

Have written Mike hope his cold is better

28, King Street
Bude
Nth Cornwall

20/10/55

My dearest Christopher,

It's not nearly post-time again & here I am with no letter written – and I haven't written Barbara yet.

So glad darling that your lectures went O.K. Had a letter from Mike.

We've had about 3 days gale - & very cold but today the sun is shining.

Fraid I have very little time on my hands – not that I'm doing anything much – but my aunt talks 15 to the dozen for hours on end & by the end of it one doesn't feel like doing anything as strenuous as pen-pushing.

You could send a *D.M.*[*Drunk Man*] to Mrs Dott[168] – in an envelope & seal it down with 4D stamps. No invoice. She'll send the money for it.

I've settled the *D. Worker* a/c – I quite thought it was finished.

I'm sending off a parcel address[*ed*] to self – do not open – as it is only odds & ends of clothing.

Do hope you are managing O.K. & that you were not too harassed with Robert & Winnie. How's the cat?

Will write a longer letter next week & let you know which day I start my travels.

Give my love to Isabel & Norman - I listened to the third programme the other night.

All my love
Christopher — my sweet

Valda X

PS Enclosing £1.

168 Mrs Mary Dott, Scottish Nationalist.

28, King Street
Bude
Nth Cornwall

Tuesday 12.15 pm

Dearest Christopher,
Have just ¼ hour to write this & catch the midday post.

Have just sent your parcel off – for you & Mike – thank you both for Christmas cards.

I'm leaving here on Monday morning 27th & will spend a night maybe two with Barbara. Will let you know there when I'm catching train probably 10 am on morning 29th or 30th – getting into Edinburgh 5.30pm. Looking forward to being back again. Hope you've been looking after yourself & that your cold has cleared up.

We've had some lovely weather but today is very cold – but not as cold of course as up north.

Haven't any news. Write send [*sic*] P.Card from London. Give my love to Mike – hope he is better.

Must run now or else I'll have to go up to the Post Office & I don't want to do that. I'll think of you both on Christmas Day

all my love

to the two of you

Valda

Enclosing £1

28, King Street
Bude
Nth Cornwall

X'mas Day.
[*1955*]

My dearest Christopher,
It is now 4 pm – wonder what you are doing dear.

We've just finished up – I'm all cleaned & prinked up. Aunt Jane is just going to do herself. She has a dreadful cold but will keep on & on.

We had a wonderful X'mas dinner – done to perfection – and a bottle of claret - I wish you could have had some.

My aunt was awfully thrilled & pleased with the flowers you & Mike sent her – she thought it wonderful.

Thank you so much for the record token. I'll enjoy getting some new records – had a letter from Mrs Jackson. She said she was bringing you up some mince and veg. Hope you haven't had too bad a time. Mrs J. was saying the weather has been very bad & that a lot of people are down with 'flu.

I get to London about 4 pm on Monday. I shall be very glad to be home again – altho' I've had a very nice time here. Today was lovely to start with – lovely sunshine but now at 4pm it has turned to rain – but nice soft gentle rain.

Think I'll drop a line to Michael. Will drop you a card from London.

Trust you managed some sort of dinner.

Just going to make the tea – I'm dying for a cup – won't be long now before I'll be home.

All my love

Valda X

POSTCARD

To Christopher Grieve, Brownsbank Cottage,
Candymill, by Biggar Lanarkshire

From Abbotsview Galashiels 9th July 1956

What a lovely [?]. Here for an hour – sure you'd love it – forgot to tell you I left Penguins flat on a shelf of new boxes in kitchen – think it the box under the coffee percolator. Hope you find them Love Valda

Brownsbank.
now in Edinburgh
Monday 3rd [*May 1957*]

Dear Christopher

Received your letter this morning – just as I was making ready to leave – managed to hitch-hike into Biggar – found the Bank closed –(a Bank holiday). Enquired at the P.O. about sending it – in Biggar – they said not. I'm in the main P.O. Edinburgh writing this & they say the same – so I'll get in touch with Drillon tomorrow – when I'm in London & explain to him your difficulties – also non-payment of pocket money etc.

Was very glad to hear from you, my dear – no! I'm quite sure I would not like Jet-plane – sounds hellish – quite a bit of bad luck being detained – thought the airport authorities would have provided you with sleeping accom. They do here – I'm (almost) sure. You're not the only one to have snow – it started at Brownsbank just before I left – but here in Edinburgh it's quite sunny. Will do my damnest to get £5 or £6 to you tomorrow . Can't do any more until I get to London – never mind about presents —

Take care of yourself. all my love Christopher dear

Valda X

Guess the country must be wonderful – what a flight – over the Gobi desert etc.

Trust you make the most of it —

POSTCARD

To Christopher Grieve, c/o Barbara Niven (Top Flat), 11, Park Hill Rise, East Croydon Nr London

From Bude Cornwall 1957

Tuesday afternoon
My dearest Christopher, Have just wired you your return fare etc. Will write you a letter tonight – but wanted you to get this tomorrow morning – which you will if I post it before 6 pm. I'd arranged to leave here on Monday morning maybe we could travel up together – will let you know times in letter – glad you are safely back again. Last two days weather has been lovely. Trust the poetry reading at the Geneva club goes off O.K. My love to Ern & Barbara. Nothing much to report this end – like you I'll be glad to be back at Brownsbank. Will definitely write you tonight & you should get it on Thursday. I believe Mike was in London today 28th flying down & back in time for work. All love Valda X

[*Postmark 1957*]
To: Christopher Grieve, c/o Barbara Niven (Top Flat),
11, Park Hill Rise, East Croydon, Nr London
From Bude

Friday

Dear Christopher,

Received your letter this morning – glad the dysentery has cleared up - & hope your gums will soon – they must be very uncomfortable – looking forward to seeing you & curious re. presents – have had no news from Michael for over a week don't know how he got on in London. If we're going to be in London until the 6th think I'll have another day here with my aunt – anyway I'll see how I manage to get packed up – as usual she has left everything (practically) for these last two days – so <u>don't</u> <u>come</u> to <u>meet</u> me on <u>Monday</u> – if I arrive will phone you at Park Hill Rise - & you can meet at East Croydon Station. Otherwise I shall definitely arrive on Tuesday catching the train 9.30 am from Bude arriving Waterloo at – I think – near enough – 3.40pm. On rereading this sounds a bit Irish – but I hope you'll sort it out. Hope it is true you're having a bit of a rest we'll need to have a little strength left for the next dog-fight – in July –

My love to you – and all

Valda x

Tuesday night [*1957*]

28, King Street
Bude
Nth Cornwall

My dearest Christopher,

I was very glad to hear you had arrived back safely – but surprised you're back before 'time'.[169] I've also been a trifle overwhelmed at the number of letters from you – so very unusual. I wired your money today as I guessed you'd be very hard-up – afraid it includes the £3-1-6 for your fare back. I've my exact fare – plus a few shillings for travelling – awful these financial details & that reminds me – I couldn't get any money to you – Barbara & Ern will vouch for that.

I also sent you four airmail letters – two addressed to the address you left me – after hearing from you & from Mike that you had not received them, I sent the last two c/o The Peking Hotel – as they did not enclosed [*sic*] money it doesn't matter. How long will you be staying in London – if you go back before me – remember that Mrs Jackson has the key – before you go up the hill – in fact it would be wiser to drop her a card, saying when you're arriving – then she could leave the key under the bucket – if you're staying a few days maybe we could go together. I'm leaving here on Monday morning, reaching Waterloo about 4pm. I'll let you know the exact time.

I think Michael should have been in London on the 28th if he could raise the £10 airfare – I couldn't help him – he was on the short leet for the East African paper & was proposing to fly down in the morning so as to be back in time for work. My aunt has failed badly – I almost feel it is too much for her to have me – poor soul she struggles on valiantly & nearly drives me to drink – fortunately there isn't any opportunity.

169 From visit to China.

Looking forward to hearing all your news – is your dysentery better and your mouth – it is so long since you had to wear your teeth for such a length of time. Just going to listen to Emlyn Williams[170]— reading Dylan growing up. Will write you again tomorrow or Thursday – hope the Geneva reading goes off O.K. & that you won't get mixed up with the B.B.C. crowd beforehand. My love to Ern & Barbara & all for yourself

Valda

---

[170] Emlyn Williams (1905-1987), Welsh playwright and actor. 'A Boy Growing Up' was a Dylan Thomas adaptation. One of the *Daily Mails* that had so alarmed Valda about the herring fishing also carried the headline 'Brilliant young author's faith in the pit' reporting how Emlyn Williams refused to watch the first night of his new play [a 'brilliant adaptation' of René Fauchois's *The Late Christopher Bean*] 'from a box or hang about the wings in evening dress after the habit of authors. Instead, in a lounge suit and old felt hat, he stood at the back of the pit, and so learned in the first 10 minutes how the play was "going over".' – *Daily Mail*, 18 May 1933, p. 16.

In July 1958 Christopher travelled to Sofia, Bulgaria with Ewan MacColl, where they met with Bulgarian writers and just generally toured the country, including the Black Sea resorts, where he was later to take Valda.

[*a.m., 31 July 1958*]
Thursday

28, King Street
Bude
Nth Cornwall

Dear Christopher,

Want to get this off by midday post so that you'll get it tomorrow if you arrive. Was very glad to hear from you – to know that you were standing up to the journey better than expected – wonderful luck for Ewan[171] — hope we manage to hear it when it comes on again. Weather hasn't been very good – today looks more promising – let me know when you expect to be back at Brownsbank so that I can warn Mrs Jackson – about the key – my aunt has really failed very badly – yesterday we had our annual row – over the cleaning of the wash-house – today everything is O.K. Janey is no trouble at all – very adjustable.

Had one letter from Mike – after about a week – all your letters are going to him – you know that. Must get this off – will write tonight or tomorrow more fully altho' I haven't anything of interest to write about. Bude is ugly just now – so full of cars & people – all my love Valda - & love to Ern & Barbara

[171] Christopher had written that Ewan MacColl had been awarded the Italia Prize of £1800 for his radio Ballad of John Axon.

July 31st [*1958*]

28, King Street
Bude
Nth Cornwall

Dear Christopher,

Received a post card from you from Varna today – wonder if you're back at Brownsbank yet – was glad to get your letter from Barbara's to know you are back again, safe & sound. You're damned lucky to get sunburnt – last week we [*had*] 4 days continual rain – have written to Mrs J. to get tobacco & things from the Co-op. I forgot to ask about potatoes – she'll get them for you, if you ask her – hope you stayed at Mike's for a few days – I'll be back next week – if it hadn't been the bank holiday weekend would have been back sooner – only it's hopeless to try & travel unless it's necessary – will let you know when I'll be arriving. Barbara is away for weekend. You've no idea dear Christopher how glad I am that you've been feeling O.K. Was really very worried – perhaps it did you lot of good. Janey has been very well behaved - & my aunt has quite fallen for her — I won't be writing again until I let you know date of arrival – find writing more than difficult here.

Michael will have told you he sent me on a cheque for £7-2-from Czechoslovakia —. I was very glad of it. I'll enclose receipt so that you can sign it. Margaret will tell Telfer about papers if you haven't already done so. You won't mind being a short time on your own – will you? Beginning of next week, would you put hot water bottle in bed – for a few days just to air the bed – Mrs Jackson said there has been a lot of rain — wonder if the cat has come back - . My aunt has really failed this time – can't think how she'll get through the winter – another thing she's taken a scunner at her neighbour – doesn't realise that people today have other interest beside housework.

Mrs Tweedie has the table bed – I told her she could have it if she wanted it before I left – now take care of yourself - & do ask Mrs J. if you want anything in the food line – don't worry about paying for things at vans etc. —. All my love darling

Valda X

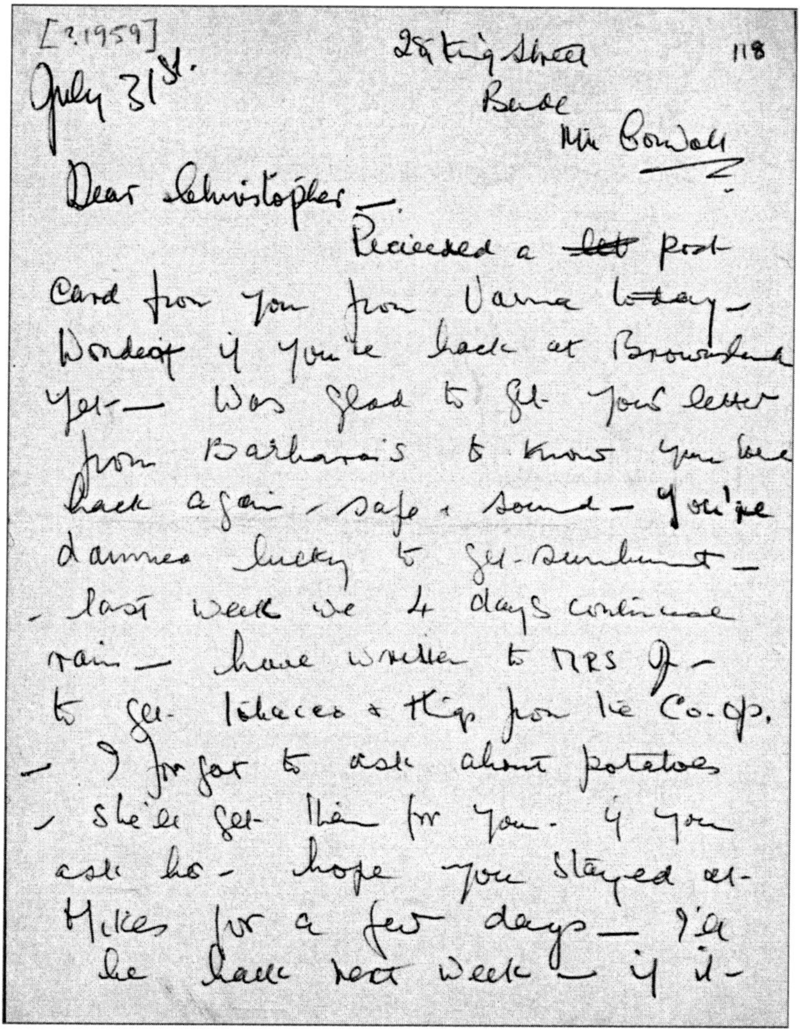

[?1959]

July 31st.

28 King Street
Bude
N. Cornwall

Dear Christopher —

Recieved a ~~let~~ post card from you from Varna today — Wondering if you're back at Brownsland yet — Was glad to get your letter from Barbara's & know you were back again — safe & sound — You're damned lucky to get sunburnt — last week we 4 days continuous rain — have written to Mrs J— to get tobacco & things from the Co-op. — I forgot to ask about potatoes — she'll get them for you — if you ask her — hope you stayed at Mikes for a few days — I'll be back next week — if it

LETTER CARD

[*Postmark Tuesday 5 Aug 1958*]

from V. Grieve 28, King Street Bude, Nth Cornwall
to Dr[172] C.M. Grieve Brownsbank Cottage Candymill, by
Biggar Lanarkshire Scotland

Monday

Dear Christopher. Will be leaving here on Wednesday – staying the night with Barbara & if all goes well will be travelling up on Thursday – the usual 10 am train. Won't hear from me again unless I decide to stay a day in London, but I don't think I will – I'm longing to be home again – do hope you managed O.K. the weather has been awful – rained all day yesterday & nearly as bad today. Will catch the bus as quick as I can after getting in

All my Love Valda X

Monday 2nd [*March 1959*]

28, King Street
Bude
Nth Cornwall

My dear Christopher,

So glad to get a letter from you. I did not write before you left because I understood you were leaving[173] on the Saturday & as I only arrived home on Thursday night well there wasn't much to say – was there? I found my aunt failed very badly indeed – a pitiful sight – altho' she has picked up quite a bit these days – with regular meals etc. – it's been a hard struggle to persuade her to go into a Home & a very cruel one – but what can one do – she really is past keeping house for herself & the next door neighbour says she can't do for

[172] Christopher had been awarded the degree of Doctor of Laws *honoris causa* by the University of Edinburgh on 5th July 1957.

[173] Budapest.

her any longer – this has hurt my aunt very much – but truthfully I cannot blame Dorothy – poor Nannie is so trying – she'd try the patience of a Saint – she drives me nearly round the bend - & I love her. I've been fitting her out with clothes & she's decided to go on Tuesday 10th – I hope we both survive by then. I'm going down by car with her & coming back the same night – if all goes well. I'm going to have a whole morning in bed after that – then I'll just tidy up the house & put things away & make one or two arrangements re keeping the house on for another 6 months – so that she doesn't feel she has burnt her boats – then I promised to go down to Truro & spend a night & go & see her all this will take about another 10 days so I won't spend more than a night in London on my way back – I'm enclosing one or two letters that have come – seeing you are almost home I haven't answered any – as a matter of fact I only wrote to Michael last night - & did not realise until today that we were into March. Murray from Alloa sent a cheque for £5 – 5 – 0 & the Whitehaven Burns Club 10-10-0 also the *Evening News* – so let me know if you want any.

We've had lovely weather & I've been sweltering in my winter clothes. I do hope you've had a lovely time – interesting etc. There has been no news from Macmillans – otherwise I would have let you know.

I think this move will just about kill poor Nannie – it's such a shame to uproot these old folks.

Will get home as soon as possible – but I must leave the place clean & tidy as she would wish it – this won't be hard once she's away & I get a decent night's rest. Dorothy will do the washing up & hard work. Do Take care of yourself once you get back to Brownsbank & don't do anything I wouldn't like you to do — So what! I told Mike to let Mrs Jackson know when you were coming back. She has a key – so has Mrs Tweedie. Give Barbara my love & Ern, if you see them this time – sorry I haven't written them - & sorry I did not write you – it's these long days without a rest that gets me down & the poor dear never stops talking she's so glad to have someone with her. Do take care of yourself dear Christopher – all my love –

Valda X

Tuesday 3rd [*March 1959*]

Dearest Christopher,

This letter came today I opened it – as I saw it came from Bulgaria – it seems if things are moving – now my sweet – it's no use your saying you'll go in a fortnight – because you really must get those papers cleared up – otherwise we'll be overrun with mice - Had a letter from Mike yesterday – the first - & not very newsy at that – today has been beautiful – only a week now before my aunt goes into a home – do hope she will bear up —

Let me know your plans – won't you – Janey sends you a tail-wag – she's awfully well behaved –

Love to you & to Mike & Deirdre[174]

Valda X

[174] Michael met Deirdre Chapman, a feature-writer on the *Evening News*, while living in Glasgow working for the *Daily Record*. They married in 1958.

28, King Street
Bude

Sunday [*March 1959*]

Dear Christopher, Mike & Deirdre — .

Had no idea that you had gone to Hungary Christopher – until Mike forwarded letters – which I got on Friday – you've certainly been having a time of it. Sorry I haven't written – but things have been far too nerve-racking. Thank God I haven't any more relations – I could never go through with it again & I'm not sure that I've done the right thing. I took her down on Tuesday 10th what a bleak unattractive part of Cornwall – have never been inland before — it was dreadful seeing her being led away by the matron – I sat on the steps & howled like a sick bitch - & when I came back & opened the door it was worse – because she has always been there.[175] Having quite busy time turning out – my aunt was as big a hoarder as you Christopher – hope to finish everything by Wednesday – then I must get cleaned up & have my hair done - & go down & see her for a couple of nights & then start for the trek North. You'll probably be at Brownsbank a few days before me. I'll only stay a night in London – seeing I've been so long down here – if you let Mrs Jackson know when you're coming she'll air the bed etc.

Thought you were a man of leisure, Mike – by now you should have more sense – going all day without food – I can see you at 35 – suffering from ulcers & palpitations & God know what – what future! I'll let you know in good time when I'll be arriving maybe we could all have meal out or something. Glad you've recovered, Deirdre – the flu' has just reached Candymill – according to Mrs J. – the yellow door sounds very attractive – will need to get our one done – before I dash off to foreign parts – don't know whether its still on – or not.

My love to you all & Fiona — .
Valda X
Did Otto recover?

---

[175] Christopher's letter from London, 20 March 1959, just returned from European tour: 'I am not going to comment about your Aunt. The whole thing is damnable. But you must not reproach yourself at all. You had no alternative in the circumstances. I do hope your visit to Truro will find her reconciled and not too unhappy. You must be completely worn-out with it all, and must certainly have a good rest here. / All my love, darling: and an extra pat or two for Janey...' – *NSL*, pp. 342-3.

Tuesday 17th [*March 1959*]

28, King Street
Bude
Nth Cornwall

My dearest Christopher,

I was so glad to get your letter today (posted March 16th). Yes, my dear – I shall be just as glad to see you again — This has been a bigger job than I thought – will only finish the cleaning of house tomorrow have closed up two bedrooms & packed all the things away nice & clean – tomorrow I'll finish the washing & ironing - & then I'm having a big clean up on myself – having my hair shampooed & set & hope to have a restful weekend – then I'm going down to Truro to see my aunt will stay one night – as the journey is complicated. They've had quite a bit of trouble with my aunt – up several nights with her – crying out for her sisters or me – feel very uncertain whether I've done the right thing or not – will probably come up to London – on Good Friday if that is suitable to Mike & start for Scotland on the Monday – if Mike & Deirdre have made other plans can stay here over the weekend as it is nice & peaceful & the rest won't do me any harm — your visit sounds very interesting longing to hear all the details — today has been bitterly cold – yesterday was lovely – hot enough to sunbathe – we've had some lovely weather – had to buy myself a little Jersey knit-costume to go to Truro – when I took down my aunt my big coat was so warm & the sun shining so bright – it looked so out of place – fancy buying a costume in Bude — I think your letters must have been chasing you – I told you in previous letter that I'd received the cheque from E.E. Lews £10-10-0 also £5-5-0 from the Alloa Journal - & £10- from the Whitehaven Burns Club I sent on the letter from the latter as thought you were expected home on the 3rd or 4th — otherwise would have answered it – have taken a note of them.

I haven't written Barbara & Ern – I've never had a minute until now to relax – had a letter from La Rue – I put her & Maisie in touch with one another – turned out very satisfactory.

I'll be glad to get back to Brownsbank believe me. Janey sends you a lick & tail wag – she has been very well behaved made friends with all the butchers. I'm on a semi-diet at the moment - to get off the extra inches.

Think the changes in arrangement that Macmillan wanted – is more interesting than a straight run through – or is it threw – also had a letter from Mrs Gray – they had called up to see us & to invite us out for a night. What are you backing for the National – I'm putting a modest 2/- each way on Mr What - & Sundown III – don't know which to pick for my third. Bought a Premium Bond on Friday 3/- My love to Mike & Deirdre & all love to yourself

Love Valda

LETTER CARD

[*Postmark Bude 11 March 1959*]

To Christopher & Michael Grieve, 34 Redcliffe Gardens, Kensington, London SW10

Sender V. Grieve, 28, King Street, Bude, Nth Cornwall

Wednesday
Wonder if you're arriving tomorrow Christopher - & how long you'll be staying in London – let me know – won't you? I'm going to Truro to see my aunt tomorrow & staying overnight – instead of going next week as intended got a chance of a lift with a policeman & his wife whose home is in Truro – so I'll probably be able to come to London on Thursday next – perhaps Wednesday let me know if either of these days are convenient – if not as I said before can stay here over weekend – don't mind being on my own at all – enjoying a bit of peace & quiet – Love to you all. Valda X

[*March 1959*]
28, King Street
Bude

My dearest Christopher,

Received your letter this morning. Glad you are home safe & sound & trust you remain all in one piece – until I meet up with you. I'll be on Wednesday – catching 9.30am from here arriving Waterloo 3.40pm if anything different happens I'll send overnight wire on Tuesday – if you hear nothing I'll arrive — on Wed.

Looking forward to seeing you all — saw my aunt on Thursday & Friday she now has a lovely little room all to herself – but is longing for the day when she can come home again. Will tell you about it.

Enclosing £5 to help along –

My love to Deirdre
Mike & yourself.

Valda X

Monday – 1pm

My dearest Christopher,

Just a note — to say I can't make Wednesday – but Thursday without fail – I could do it with an effort – the train times the same 9.35am from Bude arriving Waterloo 3.40pm on Thursday. My aunt wanted a number of things sent down to her & I promised to wash curtains & things before I left. I do hope you will wait for me - & we can travel back together – it's only a day longer – I'm enclosing a couple of letter[*s*] that came this morning.

The weather is glorious.

Hope I catch this post – give my love to Mike & Deirdre — hope she has good weather for Carnoustie — .

My love to you all —
until Thursday

Valda X

Hugh MacDiarmid's recent European trips had been very successful, 'an endless succession of lectures, talks, interviews, broadcasts and long journeys all over Hungary.'[176] *He was pleased to report to Valda an improvement in their financial situation too, with new contracts with European publishing houses and a selection of his poems coming out in Hungarian in the Spring of 1960 in addition to his payments for the tour. He had banked £100 in Budapest; consequently in the summer of 1959, Valda was able to join Christopher in Sofia, Bulgaria from where they travelled to Varna on the Black Sea coast. Christopher wrote to Michael, 'Mum has taken to the life here like a duck to water and jabbers essential Bulgarian names and phrases to the waiters quite successfully.'*[177] *On return Valda visited Cornwall again, while Christopher returned to Brownsbank.*

AIR LETTER

To Hugh MacDiarmid c/o Georgi Karaslavov, Secretary, Bulgarian Writers Union, Sofia, Bulgaria

From V. Grieve, Brownsbank Cottage, by Biggar, Lanarkshire, Scotland

Brownsbank Cottage
June 16th [*1959*]

Dear Christopher,

Received your letter from Rumania this morning also your wire – stating that you're going to Bulgaria on Saturday. Have had no word so far – but expect they are waiting until you arrive – just as well because I'll only finish all I had to do here today – apart from taking

[176] *NSL*, p. 342. Readers interested in further background to the Bulgarian part of the tour can refer to the footnote to Christopher's letter of 22 July 1959, *NSL* p. 346.

[177] *NSL*, p. 245.

Janey to Stirling etc. I don't know exactly how much Janey misses you – but I always start missing you - after a fortnight. You did not write the review for *Irish Democrat*. They want to enclose it in the next issue.

We've had very good weather. Looking forward to seeing you & hope you've had a good time in Rumania. If you have to see about the air ticket – I'll wire you if I do not receive it by Saturday – I'd really like to have next week to get Janey to Stirling, Lanark re. pension & get to London that's the 21st to end of week.

I'll get cracking now I've done all the odds & ends. Dr Tait [178] was up one night – will bring out the Photo's. Nothing appeared in the *Observer* yet – except Ferris's article on Welsh Nat. Have not seen anyone else. Enjoyed my day in Glasgow with Mike – I heard Mrs Chapman was doing a clean up – Cheers for her – . Wouldn't like to hear what she said.

Let me know per return if you want me to bring out anything – specially – I'll have quite a bit of room in my bag – it's lighter than yours. What a lot you can get on one of these air mail letters.

Think this is all – news – thought perhaps Christine Barlett would have written – no word so far – Oh dear I feel I'll never get ready – I'm just like Aunt Jane really – fiddling around doing little things – .

All my love dearest Christopher –

Valda X

Lick & tail wag from Janey

[178] The artist, film-maker & poet Dr Margaret Tait (1918-1999). Her short film study of Christopher '*Hugh MacDiarmid: A Portrait*' was released in 1964 (distributor LUX, London E8).

To the Clerk to the Trustees, The Blanchminster Trust, Bude, owners of 28 King Street.

This letter is written in Christopher's hand and uses his vocabulary, syntax, punctuation and spelling. It also shows his characteristic sloping left margin. So while it is often said Valda was very protective of MacDiarmid, the two letters in this collection (see 24/3/60 below) written by MacDiarmid on Valda's behalf reveal his protectiveness, in turn, for her.

Thank you to Mr May, present Clerk to the Trustees, who found the letters and sent the originals on. Reproduced courtesy of Deirdre Grieve, to whom more thanks are due.

Brownsbank
By Biggar
Lararkshire.
Scotland
5 – 10 – 59

Dear Mr. Chegwin.

I have only just arrived back from Bulgaria and regret that my absence has delayed payment of my aunt's rent in respect of her house at 28 King Street. I will be home in Bude at the end of the month. My aunt is coming back again and will see how she can manage by herself. When in Bulgaria I saw tamarisks which were properly kept and this confirms your view that the tamarisks in the river would have been all right if they had been properly kept.

I am enclosing herewith £6 .10/- in respect of rent due.

Yours sincerely

Valda Grieve .

[*Dec.? 1959*]
Culroy Hotel
Chapel Hill
Truro

Tuesday night

My dearest Christopher,

Have just taken my aunt back to [?] she's had a wonderful day – the weather was very good just like a spring day – we did some shopping, then came back here for lunch & stayed in my bedroom (which is very nice) until the evening meal – she thoroughly enjoyed every minute of it & I'm so glad I came down.

Had a nice weekend with Mike & Deirdre – on Saturday they did some Christmas shopping - & in the part of the evening went to the pictures & saw an old Tarzan of the Apes film – it was fun. In the evening someone was giving a party in their flat – which I did not think I'd enjoy – but did immensely – got to bed about 2.30 am had quiet day on Sunday – the journey down to here was interesting as I had not been before – .

At the party I met Tony Cronin & his wife (*X* magazine.). Did you know he was the man who argued with you at the Geneva Club that night – he came in after you had started speaking & sat with Coloquhon & MacBride. [179]

My aunt is not looking too bad.

Have decided to catch the 10 am train on Monday first – reaching Edinburgh 5.2 pm. I'll miss the 5.5 hrs – will catch the 6.15 pm. arriving home at 7.25pm. Do hope you have managed O.K. & that you're looking after Janey. Did you enjoy your dinner on Monday night.

[179] Robert MacBryde (1913-1966), artist & stage designer, attended Glasgow School of Art 1932-7 (following 5 years' work in a factory), where he met Robert Colquhoun (1914 1962), who became his close companion and associate.

Don't send any cards to the Bude folk, have sent some from here. We did my aunt's X'mas cards this afternoon.

This is a very comfortable hotel – I stayed here last time if you remember.

Altho' it's quite early, just going to wash & go to bed - & read the story of Susie Wong [180] – more interesting than the T.V. in the lounge. I sat there last night – but was bored stiff.

Look after yourself darling. I'll soon be back to bully you.

Love Valda X

[180] *The World of Suzie Wong* was a bestselling novel by Richard Mason (1919-1997) (London: Collins, 1957), later made into a film. Rather bizarrely, a 'Suzie Wong' bar and restaurant has opened in London's Soho (January 2007), where food is brought by 'waitresses dressed in Suzie Wong style dress.'

From Mr Chegwin, Clerk to the Trustees, Blanchminster Trust.

Reproduced courtesy of the present Trustees.

16th March, 1960.

Dear Mrs. Grieve,

Miss A. Rowlands,
28, King Street, Bude.

Please find enclosed herewith demand for the rent of the above property for the half year ending 25th March, 1960.

It is now just over a year ago that the trustees resolved to allow a period of six months to elapse whilst Miss Rowland went into a home without requiring her to give up her tenancy. I would be much obliged if you could now let me know what is the present position, and whether there is any liklihood of Miss Rowland returning to the house.

There is still a desperate shortage of housing which has not been made any better by the reopening of Cleave Camp, the permanent staff of which are occupying several houses in Bude and Stratton, and the fact that the trustees have a house in King Street which is not being used is causing a certain amount of adverse comment. I am afraid that it is also creating a precedent which the trustees would not wish to follow in any future cases of this kind. As I have a meeting of Trustees on Friday 1st April I wonder if you could please let me know by then what you think about the position?

Yours sincerely,
[*signed E. Chegwin*]
Clerk to the Trustees.

Mrs V. Grieve,
Brownsbank,
By Biggar,
Lanarkshire.

This reply, too, is in Christopher's hand. It is the second of two newly discovered MacDiarmid letters sent to the editor by the present Clerk to the Trustees of The Blanchminster Trust, Mr May.

Christopher's two letters and Mr Chegwin's were passed on to Deirdre Grieve, who in turn will deposit them in the National Library of Scotland, should readers wish to view these or indeed any of MacDiarmid's or Valda's letters in their repositories.

Reproduced courtesy of Deirdre Grieve.

Brownsbank, Candymill,
Biggar, Lanarkshire.
Scotland.
24/3/60

Dear Mr. Chegwin.

Many thanks for your letter of 16th inst. I now enclose the £6 .10/- in respect of rent due (for No. 28 King Street.)

I would like to thank the Blanchminster Trustees and yourself for your kindness and patience with regard to my aunt's tenancy. I appreciate this very much indeed and realize it is quite unusual in present circumstances.

The position now is that the house will definitely be opened in April when my aunt will be back there again for a trial period, as I promised her when she agreed to go into the Truro home. I would have been down ere this but for the fact that I was involved in a motor-smash and have had to be in hospital. My injuries are now healing and I will come down to Bude next month (April) as stated above. In view of this I hope your Trustees will agree to continue the tenancy until we see what this trial period does. I will inform you immediately as to that. With renewed thanks,

Yours sincerely (Mrs) Valda Grieve.

28, King Street
Bude
Nth Cornwall

4.6.60

Dear Christopher,

Sorry could not manage a letter before the weekend – things here are hectic – my aunt is playing up no end - & it's sheer hell. I'm redoubling my efforts to get her back this week – even if I have to go to the length of packing my bags – to bring her to her senses. Thank you for the wire. I hope you enjoyed yourselves at Jedborough [*sic*]– I must ask you to be careful of the pension money – I've a heavy coal bill – also Income Tax & Mrs Tweedie – then there is the Festival — so it's up to you.

I suppose poor old Nye has had it – a great pity.

Sorry about the enclosed – it got pushed behind some books & I only discovered it yesterday – I think we had last year – 52 at £4 less £16. You can work that out. The weather is still lovely altho' I'm not getting out much apart from shopping – giving Janey a ½ hour at night. Just going to scribble Mike a few lines — & that will be my correspondence for the week – unless I manage my aunt's departure.

Once she goes I'll be back as quickly as possible — .

Love

Valda X

7.7.60
28, King Street
Bude
Nth Cornwall

Dear Christopher,

So glad to get your letter this morning & sorry for not writing – but I've had so much trouble with my aunt – we'd finally settled she would go back this week – either today or Saturday. On Monday she was in a vile mood – had me in hysterics for little while – then on the Tuesday she collapsed on the floor & couldn't get up – she struggled for a couple of hours & would not let me call in a neighbour, because she was wetting all over the place. About 8pm could stand it no longer & got someone in to put her on a chair – after she had rested a while I managed to get her to the sofa - & tucked her up thinking she'd stay the night & I'd sleep in the chair – but no – about 11pm she decided she was going to bed. I tried to dissuade her – but failed. We got as far as the stairs - - of course couldn't get up – she'd lost the power of one arm – legs – so I had to roly-poly her to the rug at the fire side & there she lay all night wetting all the time – it was pathetic – finally round about 7 am I got someone in & called the Dr. he was awfully good & was here before 8 am – now she's in bed & waiting for a bed in the hospital – she'll need to go soon because I simply can't manage to lift her for the bed pan etc. – her right arm & leg - & back seems to have no feeling.

I really don't know quite what I should do – but think the best plan – although it seems harsh is – when she gets into hospital – just sell up the place – etc because it's obvious she'll never be able to come back & run the place – neither will she get anyone to look after her-. The authorities are bound to do something about it - . Most of the time she is quite clear-headed & knows what she want[*s*] – very much so – other time[*s*] she rambles a bit & talks an awful lot – she's in very good condition the Dr said & her heart not at all bad for a person of her age – so she could last long enough. If you think this is the right thing to do under circumstances – I should be back in two weeks – needing a holiday — .

I thought about you on July 2nd – glad you had a good time.

I may not have the time to write Mike this week – so will you pass this on to him – also tell Mrs Jackson. That reminds me – I'm posting a parcel to myself tomorrow - & I want you to ask Mrs Jackson to unpack it & put the things away – it's some clothes & she know[*s*] where they go. I'll try & write her myself — .

Both you & Mike talk of the new flat – but so far I do not know the address – would like it as I'll send some things direct to them – rugs etc & the mattress – as soon as I know how things are going — .

I do hope there is a bed on Saturday for her — .

What a terrible tragedy Nye Bevan passing is [181] — . My aunt was very upset over it & cried — .

Take care of yourself
Much love

Valda X

[181] Aneurin Bevan had died of cancer the previous day, 6th July, 1960.

17.7.60
28, King Street
Bude
Nth Cornwall

Dear Christopher,

I do hope all is going well at Brownsbank — do please be careful. I'd like to think I have a home to come back to. My aunt is still in hospital & doesn't seem much better. The weather is cold & windy – for which I'm thankful. On Wednesday I've arranged for the furniture to be taken away – after that I've to pick up the things my aunt wants & mine – arrange for someone to look after my aunt's affairs – clean myself up & get back as quickly as possible —

I hope to send the mattress to Mike on Tuesday – it should take only 3 days – I've sent them rugs & sheets etc. Don't open the parcels I send – unless I say so – otherwise there won't be room to move with odds & ends I'm sending on — . I'll be glad to get back & have a quiet time – I don't think I want to go anywhere - & I don't think I feel particularly loving towards anyone – I've just about had my fill. Haven't had a drink since you left – that's more than you can say – isn't it?

Janey's front feet are very bad – inflamed & swollen – I've taken her to the Vet – he thinks it was first started with tar – the beach is very bad with it – altho' I haven't been out there for the last 3 weeks. I won't be writing again until the end of the week – then I should be able to see how things are going — . If you want potatoes or anything do ask Mrs Jackson. Have you managed the Gas O.K.

There must be other things I want to say – but cannot think of them just now —

Was in seeing my aunt this afternoon – she's extremely difficult & doesn't seem to like me very much – of course it is her illness – I know that.

Tell Mike to take care of Deirdre [182] – Expect by now she'll be feeling a bit tired & emotional – I remember what a hard time I had — Take care of yourself.

Love
Valda X

POSTCARD

[*Postmark July 1960*]

To Dr C.M. Grieve, Brownsbank Cottage, Candymill, by Biggar Scotland

28, King Street, Bude, Nth Cornwall

Leaving here tomorrow Wed – travelling up on day train on Friday.

So should be at Brownsbank before nightfall –

Weather still unsettled - & the place crowded – we had the best of it –

Love
Valda

[182] Christopher and Valda's first grandchild was born in 1960. He was named Christopher.

LETTER CARD

[*March 1961*]

Hotel Bona-Vista
Meneage Road
Helston
Cornwall

Monday
8.30pm

Dear Christopher,

I arrived too late – my aunt [183] died on Sunday afternoon 2.30pm – very peacefully – they did not expect her to go so quickly – the only consolation is that if I'd travelled on the Sat. night – I'd still have been too late – as I did not get here until 5.30pm this afternoon – that's leaving by the earliest train from Paddington also she has been very confused - & wouldn't have known me anyhow — . Have just had a meal & I'm going to have a bath & go to bed – they won't get the cremation through until Thursday – won't be leaving here until the Friday for Bude – c/o Cloke 26, King Street, Bude – will get me after Friday, will write from there – Love Valda X

[183] Aunt Jane.

LETTER CARD

[*Postmark 28 March 1961*]

Monday

Dear Christopher,

I've just been to the station re trains – I'm catching 1.55 on Wednesday – missing London & going straight to Carlisle – arr. 4 AM in the morning – changing & catching Edinburgh connection arriving 7.20 – so I'lll be home 10.15 AM Thursday morning – a nice cup of tea please —. The weather has been quite good – sunny – with a cold wind - . Did you enjoy your run to Langholm - ? I hope you looked after Janey well - . All news when we meet – I'll be damned glad to be home again – give Mrs J. my love — Don't forget to be home on Thursday morning – don't want to find a locked door Much love.

Valda x

To Peter Westwater [184]

VALDA GRIEVE
BROWNSBANK
CANDYMILL. BY BIGGAR
LANARKSHIRE

8.5.62

I don't care two hoots about the bloody portrait or you – what I am concerned about is Christopher – you a friend of his – I doubt if you know the meaning of the word – Neither do I forget how you left him on the floor at Milne's a couple of years ago – This is the second time you've failed to keep your appointment – out of three sittings – I was against you painting the portrait from the beginning – as I consider you unsympathetic to Christopher politically & otherwise.

What a selfish lousy swine you are Peter –

Valda Grieve

[184] Many thanks to John Manson, for providing this letter (held in Edinburgh University Library; MS 2961.11, f. 8); he writes, ' 'Peter' was R.H. Westwater, who painted a 70th birthday portrait. Westwater rebuts Valda's accusations. He died later the same year. The portrait wasn't allowed into Brownsbank. It hung in Edinburgh University Staff Club in Chambers St.'

VALDA GRIEVE
BROWNSBANK
CANDYMILL. BY BIGGAR
LANARKSHIRE

6.8.66

To The Editor *Scottish Daily Express*

Sir: — The reference by Bailie Jack Watson of Oban, as reported in todays issue of the *Scottish Daily Express*, to the fact that Mary Wilson, mother of seven children, is unmarried is no doubt the key to the whole scandalous business of her eviction.

The fact that her name is not on the waiting list is quite evidently an afterthought. No doubt the members of Oban Town Council for her eviction are all Christians, or as Shakespeare put it "all honourable men", but in so far as they were activated by her unmarried condition it is deplorable that they did not share Christ's attitude to "the woman that had sinned", or hesitate to throw a stone before making sure they themselves do not inhabit a glass house that clearly exposes their abominable hypocrisy and lack of decent humanity.

Yours etc.

(Mrs) Valda Grieve

PS You have permission to print this letter.

V.G.

Both Valda and Christopher had visited Canada in the Spring of 1964. Christopher had agreed to do only two public engagements – one a lecture on Scottish Poetry at the University in Toronto, the other a talk to a Peace meeting – the main object being to have a much needed holiday for both and to visit Christopher's daughter Christine and her family.

Here, Valda writes during a return visit of Christopher to North America, made with the poet Norman MacCaig. MacCaig's wife Isabel, meanwhile, is staying at the MacCaig's cottage near to Brownsbank. The two men travelled via New York; Christopher wrote to Valda, 'Martin Tucker (who once visited us at Brownsbank) met us and motored us into the city. It is a long way and we had a good view of the incredible streams of traffic and the towering sky-scrapers.'[185]

[185] Evoked in Norman MacCaig's *Hotel Room, 12th Floor* and in other poems, in his *Rings on a Tree* collection published in 1968 (London: Chatto & Windus, Hogarth Press). Christopher mentioned in his letter to Valda (above) that MacCaig was staying in a room four stories above his own – *NSL*, p. 422.

Brownsbank Cottage
Candymill
by Biggar

27.4.67

My dear Christopher,

Wonders will never cease – I bet you were up at 5.30 AM - . I'm sorry to hear you're taking on more commitments – I think it's far too much for you – You know very well – we can manage quite well – we have everything we want – domestically – anyway darling – Take care of yourself –

The enclosed letter came this morning from Christine - . I'm sending it on so you can let her know your arrangement. Mrs J & I have just finished the spring cleaning – you won't know your room – All walls painted white – all [?*house*] cleaned – just a few odds & ends to clean up & then myself - I hope then to get a few days holidays – Clootie is getting on fine – I hope – yesterday she got hold of my pin cushion - & chew[*ed*] it to bits – I'm only hoping she hasn't swallowed any – Isabel is down at the cottage – We have a walk each evening. Take care of yourself.

Much love
Valda

AIR LETTER

[*Postmark 16 May 1967*]

To: Dr C M Grieve, LLD
C/o MacIntosh,
10 McIntyre Crescent, Georgetown, ONTARIO, CANADA

May 16th

My dearest Christopher – I got here yesterday – after a dreary week at St Monance – it rained all the time – not a café open – but the landlady was very kind & my digs comfortable –I suppose the sea air has done me good – on Friday Colin & Kulgin[186] came over with a Mr & Mrs Muirhead – rare book collectors & we went to the Grange Inn – St Andrews for a meal – I had a damned big steak – having been living on san[*d*]wiches & fish & chips – yesterday morning they fetched me & we went on to Helen's for coffee – it was her birthday – thought she was looking her age[187] – arrived back about 1.30pm the boys went off right away as they were expecting another couple at 5.30pm Can't say I was sorry to be back – It poured all day yesterday & today. Mrs J said it's been like that all the time – she was thrilled to get a pc from you – how very thoughtful - . Clootie was very well behaved – only a couple of mishaps – which fortunately I managed to mop up - . That my love is all my news – Yours sounded terrific – I'm so very glad everything went off so well – sounded like a grand triumphal march - .

---

[186] Colin Hamilton and Kulgin Duval, who published special editions of MacDiarmid's work (see *NSL*, p. 540).

[187] Helen Cruickshank is now 81.

2

There's quite a bit of correspondence here – but nothing of importance – things that can wait – have no word from the Library people [188] – I'm seeing Mike on Sunday – the family are coming out for lunch – he told me about the cheque – You remember Bill Henry (Henry Stuart) the painter fellow – who came out with my bête noir David Morrison – he died from a heart attack.[189] Mike was telling me a fantastic tale of you changing your money into 1 dollar notes & stuffing them in your briefcase – dear God you must have felt like a gangster and 10 ft tall - . I explained to Mike that it was probably originally my fault – as I'd asked you [*to*] bring home some dollars – I think you'd better change it into travellers cheques – we can then change them at the American Express - & they don't through the bank unless you can think of a better way – but don't stint yourself – have a good time. I'm also glad you're going to have a proper check-up – I think your insurance covers you for 21 days Will you let me know in good time what time you're expected at Prestwick – Colin said he'd come for me & we'd meet you & bring you out here – Expect you'll be

3

tired — I'm surprised at you getting snow – remember the lovely weather we had — Give my love to all the family – Barker & Humphrey Milne – I hope to see them all again some day. Some more proofs came in from McGibbon & Kee – Mrs J sent them on to Mike - & last night on the phone he said he'd got them away - .

Can't think of anything else – anyway I must run down to the post if I'm to get it away today – much love to you all – especially you

Valda

[188] This may refer to plans for a special exhibition at the National Library of Scotland to mark Hugh MacDiarmid's 75th birthday.

[189] Bill Henry, that is. At the time of writing this note, David Morrison is living in Wick.

Brownsbank Cottage
Candymill
by Biggar
22/5/67

My dear Christopher,

Many thanks for your letter May 15th – you've certainly kept me well-posted – thank you.

Now to answer your various questions – American Channel 13 TV cheque arrived a couple of days ago 230 dollars also your STV cheque £38 odd. Your books have not arrived yet —. Sounds as if you're having a wonderful time. I like the way you speak casually of flying here and there – darling it's hard to imagine – when catching a bus here is an effort - .

The weather is foul rain & bitterly cold – on Wednesday we had snow.

I've been home this past week & damned glad – haven't been to Langholm or to Torrs now it's too late. Tomorrow I'm going to Mike's for a couple of days – also have a Border terrier show at Lanark & one in Biggar June 3rd. I've sent photo's to McGibbon & Kee – also one to Tom Scott for *Agenda* – The only person I've seen is Boothby so I haven't been pestered – which has been marvellous after all the visitors we've had - .

Looking forward to seeing you on Tuesday – beginning to weary for you now – it's been a good break. You'll have got my letter asking for the time of your flight – now just a small – very small rebuke for spoiling your very nice last letter with irrational irritability concerning Norman [190] – you must realise he was under considerable pressure from me – Mike and a lot of other people to look after you. We were all very worried after the bad attack you had at the Burns Supper and at Milnes – I know you're an isolationist willingly or not I don't know – but we're not all built that way so do have a sense of

[190] *NSL*, p. 425 – likely refers to Christopher defending himself regarding the money stuffed into cases: he is quite capable of looking after himself and does not require supervision of this kind, he writes; Norman MacCaig was over-zealous at times in Christopher's company and 'is in some respects an abominable fuss-pot and like all teachers apt to be very dictatorial.'

humour, my love — You've cried wolf a great many times – perhaps this isn't quite the right metaphor – but you know what I mean.

Mike [*h*]as been asked to stand for the SNP in two constituencies — Elderslie & Govan – the first is out because of Norman Buchan – the latter he's considering. [191]

I'm enclosing snap for Christine -. Give them all my love

Much love

Valda X

[191] J.M.T. Grieve later stood for the SNP in Govan, in 1970. He came third with 2,294 votes (10.3%) – my thanks to Mhairi Hunter of the SNP Policy Unit for taking the trouble to look this up.

Christopher returned from Ontario at the end of May 1967. Whilst Valda was away, he stayed with Mike and Deirdre in Glasgow. The 1969 letter is written while Christopher is attending the wedding in Canada of Christine's sister-in-law Sheena. 'The Lakes' refers to Christine and her husband Alistair's holiday house which they built on an island in Lake Muskoka. [192]

POSTCARD

[*Postmark 16 September 1967*]

from Cala Millor, Mallorca to Dr C.M. Grieve & family
c/o 7, Hamilton Drive, Glasgow W. Scotland

Sunday
Arrived here 6.30 am on Sat. morning. I crawled up for breakfast or rather cup of teas [?]. Feeling much more relaxed – quite a quiet place – with a nice breeze from the sea – writing this on the balcony (very good one just on the sea front no need to go down among the crowd) and sipping a [?] Trust you've weathered your activities successfully. The village is [?] miles away – expecting today to get our bearings. Everything closed today being Sunday – almost as bad as Scotland.
Take care,
Love

Valda & Jane

192 Thanks to Deirdre Grieve for this information.

Brownsbank Cottage
Candymill
by Biggar
27/6/69

My dearest Christopher,

You've been gone just over a week & it's about time I had a chat with you —

Going into Lanark last Saturday (21st) to the Dog Show I remembered I hadn't put in your kilt pin – I'm sorry – but I guess you managed somehow – and Mrs Jackson dreamt you went to the wedding with the [?*tacknap*] still in your kilt - .

There's been very little mail – a couple of people wanting you to read their poems & until today – that's about all – Got your record from Claddagh[193] – and have just been playing it – very good indeed – it's the one with the shorter poems - . The sleeve is terrific – red with a large photo of you doing your commercial laugh - .

Hugh & Pat[194] came down on Wednesday afternoon & stayed overnight – Hugh cut the grass & at night we went to the Hart-tree Hotel & had a meal – all very sober & proper – I had a bad attack of Diverticululus (can't spell it) so I did nothing out of the ordinary — .

All was fine until we got back then Pat started sloshing it back - & ended after numerous falls – to start capering around the place stark naked - . Hugh & I managed to get her safely in the dormandbule (another word I can't spell)[195] – it was like lassoing a young steer - .

[193] 'Hugh MacDiarmid reads his own poetry,' recorded in Ireland by Peter Hunt Studios, Dublin, November 1968 for Claddagh Records; sleeve notes by Alexander Scott, who can now describe MacDiarmid as 'Scotland's greatest living poet, and arguably the very greatest of all the makars who have written in the Scots tradition...also one of the great poets of the world, for he has succeeded in his early aim to 'aye be whaur extremes meet' and his work is both national and international...'

[194] 'Hugh Paton and his wife Pat had a farm at Auchencairn near Kilquhanity School. They became close friends of the Grieves.' (Deirdre Grieve, corresp.)

[195] Mis-spellings are of diverticulitis and Dormobile (a camper van), respectively.

They went off on Thursday morning in quite good fettle - . In the afternoon Kulgin & Colin arrived & we had a very nice time playing records – Colin cooked (just had a phone call from Mike – everything OK) a chicken in butter & lemon juice – shrimp cocktail – strawberries & cream & a bottle of wine – Mungo the deerhound was here – he's about a foot above the table - . This morning we went into Peebles for coffee - & had a look round – met Nan McLellan & Mrs Walker[196] – the latter had been staying for 3 days at the Hydro. George & his family are home from Canada - & treated the old lady – she's 85 & still very lively - . Sad news – that little bitch Clootie hasn't had any pups – I'm furious – so she's on starvation diet — after me feeding her up – no more titbits from you – either - . I can hear your laughs - .

In case you're thinking I'm having too good a time – it took me a week & a day to do the spring cleaning – thought I was never getting to the end of it — .

This is all the news here – what about you – trust the wedding went off in good style - & that you didn't run off with the bride - .

The weather here has been hellish – it rained for a whole week - & this week hasn't been much better – I do hope you're having a rest up on the Lakes – I'm dropping Christine a note but I'll enclose a couple of snaps for her – of Lucien[197] & Mike – Make the most of your holiday & have a rest – no need for you to be back here – until the July 8th or 9th

Your room looks very orderly & empty without you — .

Much love

Valda

[196] Agnes Walker, again.

[197] Christopher and Valda's second grandchild, born 1964. A third grandchild, Dorian, was born in 1973.

Christopher was hospitalised in 1969. Once discharged, he resolved to cut down on the number of his public engagements; however, in the New Year he travelled to Ireland and East Germany, holidayed with Valda in Provence and Italy and continued travelling throughout the UK giving poetry readings, interviews and fulfilling other public commitments.

POSTCARD

[*Blank postcard, postmark 18 Nov 1969*]

To: Dr C M Grieve
Chalmers Hospital, Lauriston Place, Edinburgh

17/11/69

Dear Christopher,
I've found the typescript of *The Threepenny Opera*[198] – and the word you were wanting ακριβώς[199] – without disturbing anything - .
We got home after 4pm – do hope everything is OK –
Will get in touch with Kulgin tomorrow
Much love
Valda

[198] In February 1972 he would write to Edwin Morgan, '... there are elements in Brecht with which modern English can't deal – for which it is far too refined. These elements are nearer elements in Scots, e.g. in Dunbar and Burns.' – *NSL*, p. 467. MacDiarmid's translation of Brecht's *Threepenny Opera* was published by Methuen in 1973.

[199] The Greek adverb means 'exactly', 'precisely' (Deirdre Grieve, corresp.).

WORLD WILDLIFE FUND PANDA CARD

[*1969*]

Sunday night

Dear Christopher – I'm jolly glad you are in hospital all snug & warm. We've had a blizzard today & it's been bitterly cold – so different from yesterday – it was beautiful in Edinburgh – we went down town & had lunch at one of these "whole-meal" places – got home at 4.30pm by that time the frost had started & the house was like a 'fridge – I'll be thinking of you tomorrow morning & trust everything goes well. I've heard you have had a few visitors already - .

If there is anything important in the mail I'll get it to you right away.

Today I've had a lazy day – can't say I feel any the better for it –

Take care of yourself – it will be nice to have you back

Much love

Valda X

WWF PANDA CARD

[*Not dated, 1969*]

Monday night

My dearest Christopher –

I waited until today to write you in case there was anything in the mail – nothing that needed an immediate answer - . Mike probably told you I had a nice day with the Frizzell's[200] – but what a homecoming a near blizzard - & bitterly cold – took me hours to warm up – the house was like a Fridge- . As you know I phoned up today & they said you'd be in for another couple of days – be thankful that you are snug and warm. It's good that things are no worse – I'll see the Dr when I come in to fetch you. Alex McCrindle[201] phoned yesterday & Edward Nairn[202] tonight – they are coming out next week before they go down to Peter[?] – Thank goodness there is no news – that needs any attention. I'll be glued to the telly tomorrow afternoon – the Budget[203] – expect you'll be listening as well.

I'll be having an early night – I hope tonight – have a habit of [?*dawdling*] on –

Look after yourself & do as you are told –

Much love

Valda X

---

200 Second-hand bookshop proprietors.

201 Alex McCrindle, (1911-1990), actor and Equity organiser. His second wife was the children's author Honor Arundel.

202 Also a bookseller.

203 The Budget in 1969 had been surrounded by controversy regarding prior leaks of information by a Conservative MP; it was thought that car tax did not rise in this year's budget due to this leak.

On August 11th 1971 Christopher was preparing to celebrate his 79th birthday when his health deteriorated 'very suddenly.... My daughter, son-in-law, various grandchildren were all here and we were going out to celebrate. Instead I was rushed into an Edinburgh hospital. So I'm not counting that birthday – my next is not my 80th but still my 79th. The surgeon (and my son-in-law who is a consultant physician in Canada) both insisted that there was no need for me to cancel the arrangements I was making to go to the USA and Canada about 25th October.... They said I was fitter to go now than I'd have been before being operated on.'[204] *Although still claiming to be restricting his public engagements, he did admit to his daughter Christine that 'as in a quicksand the more you struggle to get out of it the more hopelessly you become involved.'*[205]

[15 *August* 1971]
Sunday night

Dearest Christopher—.

I'll be thinking very much about you on Tuesday – I can only hope things won't go too badly - .

The weather is getting worse – very strong winds - & damned cold – Had a very good time yesterday – I didn't know so many little second-hand book-shops existed & made a living – was in one yesterday – small & shabby – yet a few weeks ago the owner sold over £2000 worth of books to one buyer – incredible.

If any important letter[*s*] come I'll get them to you –

Keep cheerful – don't let things get you down –
All my love darling
Valda X

[204] Letter of 14 September 1971, *NSL* pp. 460-2.

[205] Letter of 1 February 1973, *NSL* p. 479.

[16 August 1971]
Monday night

Dear Christopher –

I rang up this evening asking for you. I hope you got the message – because foolishly I forgot to give my name –

I'm glad you are having a blood transfusion – thought you should have had it the last time.

You will have got all the news from Mike on Sunday – we had a very nice day – quite fruitful – re grass cutting –

Young Christopher goes back tomorrow – he's worked very well - & it's been nice having him .

No mail of any consequence. Willie Johnstone rang up & rambled on – and on – it seems he'll have something to show soon — that is if he doesn't fiddle around with his very important – bloody lithographs – Christopher's gone to bed - & I'm just going – we've both worked hard today –

Much love, my dear –

Valda X

Dear Christopher,

Your Dinner is on the range – a loaf of bread in the tin in the scullery – 1/ on the dresser & 1/ in the little desk.

Eat up the bannocks in tin first

please take care of yourself, & don't behave silly –

Love
Valda

Put milk bottle out on Monday night & each of the following nights – but not on Sunday night.

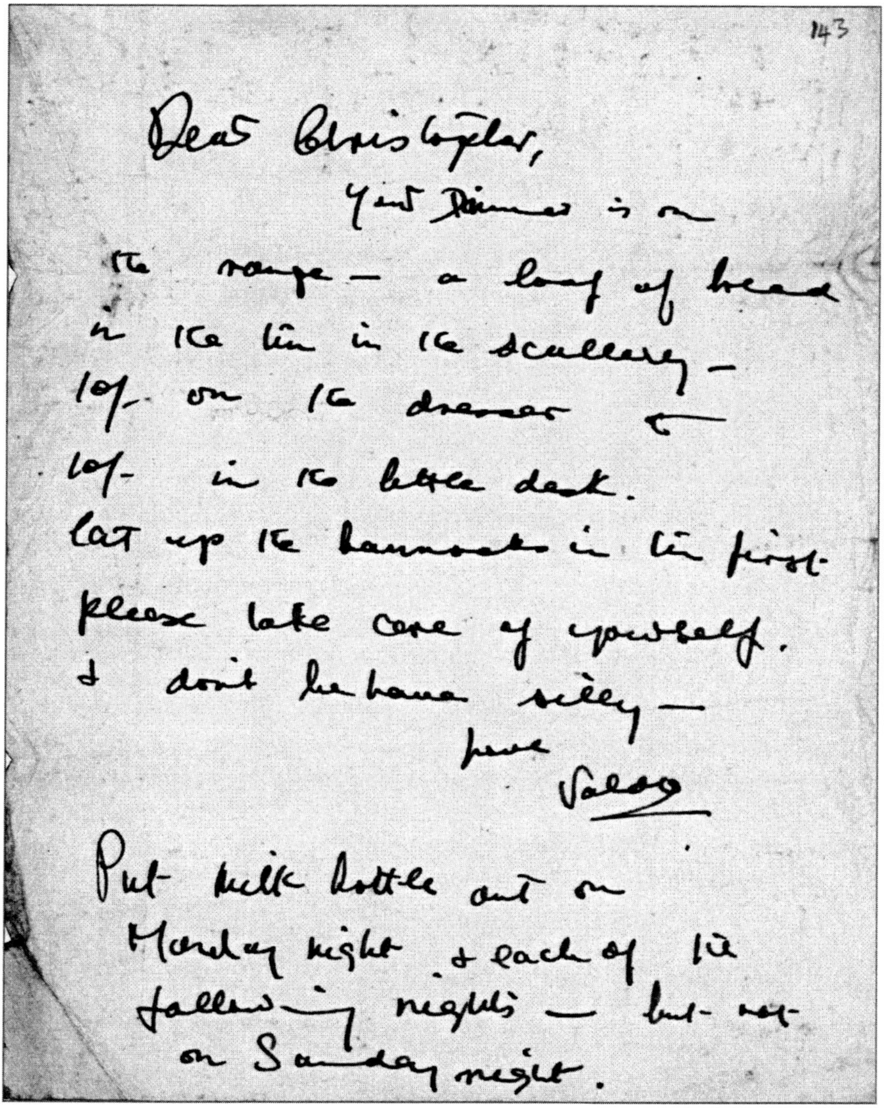

143

Dear Christopher,

Your dinner is on the range — a loaf of bread in the tin in the scullery — 10/- on the dresser & 10/- in the little desk.

Eat up the bannocks in the tin first.

Please take care of yourself & don't be a silly —

love

Valda

Put milk bottle out on Monday night & each of the following nights — but not on Sunday night.

POSTCARD

[*Postmark Romania 25 September 1972*]

Sunday 24th

Been here a week – spent most of the time sleeping – going to bed at 8 pm – now down with tummy bug. Weather warm – coolish wind hotel & food good – too many bloody W. Germans for my liking – not liked here by Romanians – difficult to explain difference. Money disappearing like snow of[f] a dyke – we haven't been out for a drink at night – Wouldn't come here again – Jane is already repacking to go home. Hope you're enjoying yourself. Much love Valda

In Autumn 1975 Christopher sustained injuries falling down a stair in Michael's house in Glasgow, necessitating an eye operation in November. 'I was lucky not to break any bones, but I was unlucky in being sober, since with drink taken I'd have fallen more lightly,' he wrote.[206]

LETTER CARD

[*November 1975*]

To: Dr C M Grieve
C/o (Men's Ward 4) Chalmers Hospital
Lauriston Place, Edinburgh

From Valda at Brownsbank Cottage

Tuesday night

My dearest Christopher,
I 'phoned up this afternoon – I didn't realise you hadn't had your op. If the injection eases your pain – that's all to the good. I hate to think of you suffering and I can do nothing to help.
Anyway you'll be warm & cosy – that[*'s*] more than we are here – On Sunday night we had a very bad snowstorm – continues off & on – during Monday - & today suddenly the room became quite dark – the snow came down so thick – you could not see through it - & then it was brilliant sunshine - . Nothing of any importance so far in the post. I expect you'll be out on Saturday – if not I'll try & get in to see you – you know Lucien is coming up on Friday – I think Mike said tomorrow should see the end of "operation cleaning up" & I'll have a day's rest
All my love – I'll be thinking of you   Valda. Xxx

---

[206] To William Johnstone, *NSL* p. 497.

In Christopher's latter years, he and Valda were seldom separated. Christopher wrote, '- in fact I need [Valda] nowadays to get about safely.'[207] *They travelled together throughout the UK; to Holland, Ireland; to Canada once more in 1976.*

Christopher endured 6 operations throughout 1977 as well as a course of radiotherapy as treatment for a rectal tumour. Valda and James Michael were cognisant for some 6 months before Christopher of the fact this was cancer.

Christopher put his affairs in order in a letter to Michael of 12th June 1978. Despite having been housebound since the beginning of that year and in pain, by sheer force of will it would seem, he travelled with both Valda and Michael to Ireland again to receive an honorary degree from the University of Dublin on 6th July.

Christopher Murray Grieve died on 9th September 1978, aged 86. He was buried in Langholm, the town of his birth.

---

[207] To Geoffrey Bridson, *NSL* p. 484; also to other correspondents.

Valda's letter of acknowledgement after Christopher's funeral, sent to several, usually with a personal line or two added. Christopher had corresponded with James Caird from their Whalsay days.

Brownsbank, Candymill, by Biggar, Lanarkshire

Sept 1978

Dear James & Janet Caird,

Many thanks for your kind letter regarding Christopher. His death, although expected, has been a severe blow. Apart from his courage and wit to the end, he always seemed so indestructible.

Many messages have flooded in, and they reveal an undoubted sense of loss, well summed up in the *Scotman*'s first leader which started: - "Scotland seems a colder quieter place ..."

I hope, with all my heart, that what he stood for will not only be remembered, recognised and built-on in terms of the Scottish Renaisance, but also fought for on the political front until his long-held aim is achieved and Scotland is once again independent and capable of deciding its own destiny.

In the past few days, and at the funeral at Langholm, it was particularly heartwarming to acknowledge and re-discover the wide-ranging love and regard that he was held in by so many individuals and representatives of diverse movements.

Sincerely

Valda Grieve

I'm glad you were able to come & see him & so was he — .

Dear Alan Bold, Alice & Valentine,

[*as above*]

Sincerely
Valda

Thank you for your very sensitive article in the *Scotsman*. V.

From Sam Gilliland[208]

10/10/82

108 Overtoun Rd.
Springside, Irvine
KA11 3BW

Dear Valda,

Once again I enjoyed our visit, and thank you for making us feel 'at home'. Norman MacCaig was splendid at our poetry festival and hopefully we can make the event an annual one. We have been approved as tenants for the new 'Burns' centre in Irvine so that will help the club immensely – you know enough of me to be assured that the place will not be a dead museum. Gerry and I were arguing (in the nicest way) over a point we discussed whilst with you concerning Dylan Thomas' death. My understanding was that he was already being treated with antibiotics before he went out and returned 'under the weather' and that against doctors' advice, his subsequent asthmatic attack was again treated but he did not respond.

[208] Secretary of the Scottish International Open Poetry Competition.

2

I would be deeply grateful if you could clear the matter up for us before either I punch Gerry on the nose or he baps me one.

Well Valda, we are heading into another winter again and I hope this time you find things a little easier. If there is anything we can do for you before the roads become impassable, please do not hesitate to let me know. Sometimes my dear I envy you your solitude, but at other I realise the inner loneliness that you feel. I will telephone from time to time and trust that the long winter night will pass by quickly. At least I'll get some writing in – hope to hell some publisher will print the stuff! Sorry about my terrible scrawl, never could improve on it.

Warmest love,
Sam

To Sam Gilliland

Dear Sam Will you give this to Gerry – don't know his address. Re the death of Dylan Thomas — he was staying with a friend of friend of mine – she let him out for a drink – failed to tell the Dr – because she was afraid – and the infection killed him – Tragic —.

V.G.

[*Envelope: in Sam Gilliland's hand*]
Alan.
Enclosed is a letter from Valda Grieve, widow of Hugh MacDiarmid, in response to my our [*sic*] letter regarding the death of Dylan Thomas. This has still not been made public and must be treated with discretion!

To Sam Gilliland

POSTCARD

[*Postmark Glasgow 19 July – year not visible*]

Dear Sam — sorry not answering your letter Have been in hospital – with another stroke – Dammitt affected my speech – very frustrating – and my writing. Going to Langholm on Wed. for 10 days will write when I get back. Certainly you may use the poem – if you think it good enough – best of luck with the new magazine.

Love to you & the family
Valda

To Lucien Grieve and Jenny [209]

Brownsbank Cottage

14/1/87

Dear Lucien & Jenny

Belated New Year's Greetings & may everything (or nearly all) your wishes come true. I gather you're enjoying yourselves – despite the "hard" work. Try & get as much out of it as you can – even their hanging about Glasgow. As usual I went to Glasgow for Christmas on X'mas day we went to the Semple's for a morning drink, champagne & smoked salmon sandwiches. Back for lunch Deirdre had cooked a 20lb turkey with all the trimmings & then we sat down at that long, long table – only – the 4 of us bunched at one end – it was rather sad. Christopher [*grandson*] had been home for 10 days — but was recalled 2 days before Christmas. I came back here for the N. Year – thought it was better not to be too dependent – had quite a good time – went into Biggar on N. Years Eve & saw the Bonfire – it was a lovely night clear & bright – they had a lovely old fair-ground organ playing with brightly painted puppets. Since – things have been fairly quiet – we've had some really nice weather – that's over now its been snowing gently for nearly a week – the lane is still clear – that's because we've had no wind – I hope you'll enjoy the book I bought several copies & sent them to friends who are inclined to [?] Mrs Thatcher (not you)

I've had some really – phone calls – left me laughing – the drawings are very good – don't you think?

Family news – M & D have had to move the caravan – They were up this weekend – the whole business is so stupid – they can put a hut on the land – but not the caravan. SHIT. Dorian got a <u>very</u> good school report – the first in the family. Mike is having to go to the hospital today to find out what's wrong with his throat – he can scarcely speak – he's had it now for nearly 4 months & is getting

[209] Lucien's then girlfriend, with whom Lucien had travelled around the world for two years (Deirdre Grieve, corresp.)

worse – keep your fingers crossed. He went in this morning – I'll hear what is happening tonight - & let you know.

The *Collected Poems* in paperback by Penguin is coming out in Feb. No word yet when the sculpture is going up – it's finished – that's another cock-up.

Jenny – Deirdre & Dorian each had a card from your Gran at Christmas. When I left Deirdre was going to ask her over.

Jake is turning out to be a really nice dog – he now sits outside a shop & waits.

Can't think of anything more news – besides my writing getting worse – I still find it difficult. I hope you can read most of it.

My love to you both

Valda xx

Thanks for your letter – snaps – was so pleased to get them.

Just had a 'phone from Mike – he['s] home & has to go in on Thursday – to have a probe put down his throat. So far so good.

James Michael Grieve developed cancer of the larynx. He died in 1995.

From a notebook of Valda's, 'Nature Study' – frontispiece reads "Without category – I suppose that means odd bits & pieces".

Christopher
It was a touch & go venture, liable to end in shipwreck.

—

We both made sacrifices ourselves, Christopher sacrificed himself – for his principles & I sacrificed myself for Christopher

—

Became a legend in his life time.
Hard / easy to live with.
For the little time I've had with you. Thank you!

—

Suppose I'll be haunted by the ghost of MacDiarmid — I don't want to lose Christopher Grieve.

—

I've said somewhere before need is more lasting than love.

—

I don't believe in making a conscious effort to change a person from the person you married – that usually destroys a marriage.

—

I cannot understand people who give up on life – just self indulgence – the only thing to do is to cope with it – so I cope not always too well.

Extract from a Last Will and Testament, dated 1/11/78, i.e. soon after Christopher's death.

The Last Will and Testament of Valda Trevlyn Grieve of Brownsbank Cottage, Candymill, Biggar
to Michael Grieve and Deirdre Grieve, Executors

. . . I want to be buried beside Christopher in Langholm Cemetery, the service to be non-religious and conducted by Campbell MacLean of Crammond Kirk –
No shrouds – but with a dress or trouser suit – and a brassiere - !
Valda Trevlyn Grieve

Witnessed by JM White of Langholm and by Norman MacCaig

Valda Trevlyn Grieve died, suddenly, at Brownsbank Cottage on 23rd May 1989, aged 82.

The Scotsman of 25th May carried the headline, '*Inspiring force behind the poet*'. Raymond Ross wrote: '... As wife, companion and champion of her husband's work, she remains part of the Scottish literary Renaissance: the woman who helped MacDiarmid pick up the pieces after the disastrous breakdown of his first marriage, who saw him through his own nervous breakdown and who kept him together body and soul during the hungry thirties in virtual exile on the island of Whalsay in Shetland – as well as during the bleak war years of conscripted labour on Clydeside...'

Appendices

Appendix I:
Structure of MacDiarmid's Sentence

This syntactic analysis is provided by Dr Lucy Dipper, Department of Language and Communication Science, City University, London, to whom thanks are due.

MacDiarmid's words are presented in this typestyle, Dr Dipper's analysis the contrasting style.

This is one sentence, containing the main verb (was) which has scope over the whole sentence.
Was is a form of the copular verb ***to be*** which forms a verb phrase (VP) with a list of conjoined adjective phrases (APs):
i.e. [**V** [AP] conj [AP] conj [AP] conj [AP]]VP :

[I] – subject NP
[was – copular verb
[absolutely down-and-out at the time – with no money behind me at all] - AP , (conj)
[broken down in health] - AP , (conj)
[unable to secure remunerative employment of any kind] - AP , and (conj)
[wholly concentrated on projects ...*] - AP since (conj)

* The noun phrase (NP) which is headed by the noun (N) ***projects*** is itself a complex structure containing many conjunctions.
projects in poetry and other literary fields **which (conj)** could bring me no monetary return whatever , **(conj)** involved continuous intense effort ridiculously out of proportion to my strength **,and (conj)** called for facilities, **(conj)** in the way of books ,**(conj)** papers **, and (conj)** even intercourse – the friction of mind upon mind

Since is a subordinating conjunction which joins the following subordinate clause to the final conjoined NP (headed by intercourse, see above)
[[isolation] and [a too complete self-centredness]] – subject NP
were – copular verb
[definitely dangerous, **not only (conj)** to the qualities of the work to be produced **but (conj)** to my own mental stability **or, if scarcely that** – for if I had been capable of developing any form of insanity, I would certainly have carried myself irrevocably over the border line long ago – **at least** to the generation and maintenance of the necessary, or at any rate the most helpful, mood] -AP

Dr L. Dipper

Appendix II:
Valda's Family in King Street, Bude

The houses and cottages in King Street, Bude, including number 28, were owned by The Blanchminster Trust for the entire period covered in this book. The Blanchminster Trust is one of Cornwall's oldest charities, going back over 500 years. The Trust's aims are to provide relief for those in the community who are in need, hardship or distress, and to promote the education of those resident in the area of the former Bude-Stratton Urban District.

The land on which the King Street properties were built was given to the Charity in 1421. In her history of the Blanchminster Trust, Kathleen Beswetherick writes:

> *Little is known about the builders of the houses in King Street apart from the fact that Richard Bevan built several cottages on the west side about 1830. ... There is a suggestion that many of the cottages were built for workers engaged by the Bude Canal Company and the name King Street may have been given in recognition of the canal's most distinguished customer, Captain King, an officer in the Royal Navy. An alternative suggestion is that some cottages were built in the reign of William IV and were lived in by 'his men,' that is, the Excisemen.*

67 houses and cottages in King Street acquired by the Trust in the late nineteenth century were said to have been 'in a most dilapidated condition and almost wholly unprovided with sanitary requirements' and a considerable amount was spent on repairs. In 1926, when re-roofing was required, the walls were not stable enough to hold new slates, so were patched with old slates at the front and asbestos tiles at the back. When Kathleen Beswetherick wrote her history in 1991, she noted, 'The King Street properties continue to be a problem and are constantly undergoing repair.'

Some twenty years ago, a number of the properties in King Street, including number 28, were sold on the open market. When it transpired that some of these were used only as holiday homes (not 28), the sales were stopped, so that the houses and cottages may continue to benefit people in the local community.

It was very difficult indeed for Valda to see her last surviving aunt give up tenancy of their home in King Street. The England Census Record for 1891

shows that Valda's family had lived in King Street for at least three generations. Valda's grandmother Mary Rowland (b. Poughill, abt. 1851, d.?1919) is recorded in the 1891 Census as living in number 25 King Street as a widow with five children, all of whom were born in nearby Stratton. Her children were:
Maud Mary Rowland, aged 19 at the date of the Census,
Florence Rowland (to become Valda's mother) aged 11,
Agnes Rowland (to become one of Valda's aunts) aged 9,
Samuel Rowland, aged 5,
and George Rowland, aged 4.

In addition, a widow named Hannah Coombe, aged 46 on the Census date, was also resident with the Rowland family.

A Samuel Rowland, senior, is recorded in the Rent Records of King Street (held by the Blanchminster Trust) as being a tenant in 1889. It is likely, therefore, that he passed away between 1889-1891. Mary Rowland is then recorded as the tenant, until 1919.

No 'Jane Rowland'as such can be found in either the Census or Rent Records.

28 King Street, today (second door from right).

Appendix III: The Gilgal

Extracts from
The One Hundred and Fourth Annual Report of James Murray's Royal Asylum Perth

REPORT of the PHYSICIAN-SUPERINTENDENT for the Year ending 31st March, 1931.

... The most important incident in the course of the year has been the completion and occupation of a new detached hospital block named, after the property on which it is situated, Gilgal Hospital.... For many years the Murray Royal and other Royal Mental Hospitals of Scotland have received and treated and restored to health a large number of early and mild cases of mental and nervous disorder, and have earned the gratitude of innumerable patients and their friends. It is, however, apparent that many such invalids are deterred from availing themselves of proper care and treatment by a fear, not always unfounded, that they might in doing so be brought into close contact with patients more seriously ill than themselves, association with whom may be distressing and disagreeable. A sympathetic appreciation of the wishes and needs of such discriminating patients has led the Directors to provide the special accommodation now available to the public, in Gilgal Hospital.

This hospital will be reserved entirely for voluntary patients and especially for those whose malady is slight or of short duration, who are sensitive and fully appreciative of their surroundings and company, and who are apprehensive of possibly harmful or painful contacts with invalids of a more confirmed or different type.

.... Gilgal Hospital has therefore been erected and opened to the public with a certain definite object....I have very little sympathy with the movement which is so apparent in recent years and which might be termed by analogy the "flight from the (word) asylum." The atmosphere and environment in an ordinary Asylum are by no means necessarily more distressing and painful or disagreeable than those of any hospital, and I am constantly struck with the fact that those suffering from mental disorders are much more tolerant of the symptoms and ways of their associates than are the patients in a ward of a General Hospital. I admit, however, that there are many patients who need special treatment and skilled nursing which they cannot get at home and who for sound or for sentimental reasons are reluctant to enter an Asylum or Mental Hospital even as voluntary boarders, and for this type hospitals such as Gilgal may prove to be the solution of their difficulties.

The attitude of the average citizen towards mental disease and mental hospitals in particular has always been one of deep distrust and aversion, arising probably from some obscure ramification of the Herd instinct. In the past, however, when an individual had the misfortune to suffer a mental breakdown he was promptly dealt with, certified in due form and sent to the Asylum to take his chance. Ten years ago I had occasion to complain that patients were being brought to this Institution under medical certificates, who had insight, were not seriously ill and who were eligible to enter on a voluntary status as technically sane persons. The position is now changed. Nowadays one from time to time sees a patient who is quite seriously ill and who urgently needs specialised treatment and nursing, and one is told by the relative that while they are prepared to take any steps in reason to benefit the patient, his entry to a Mental Hospital will not be considered! It is in no subservience to such foolish ideas that Gilgal Hospital has been opened.

FARM AND GARDENS:

The year passed without notable incident in the departments managed by Mr. Johnston. The various crops were of average size and were secured without difficulty. The poultry farm supplied 823 dozen of eggs. The fruit and vegetable crops were on the whole better than usual, particularly peaches and small fruit. Among other items the following were supplied to the Institution: - apples, 45 cwts.; plums, 456 lb.; gooseberries, 1212 lb.; raspberries, 1075 lb.; peaches, 623 lb.; grapes, 630 lb.; tomatoes, 892 lb.; celery, 1392 lb.; beetroot, 3275 lb.

Some levelling was done in the cricket field to improve the wickets.

...

W. D. CHAMBERS.

Notes on Gilgal Hospital

Gilgal Hospital is situated on the slopes of Kinnoull Hill about 200 feet above sea level, and its entrance gate is about one mile from Perth on the Muirhall Road, on the east side of the river. Its private rooms, verandahs and gardens face south and west, and it commands to the north a magnificent view of the valley of the Tay and the mountains beyond. It is reserved solely for voluntary patients and it intended only for those whose standard of conduct, habits, etc., is high.

The Hospital consists of two wards and a central administrative block. .... The floors throughout are of oak, the doors and other fittings of Lagos mahogany, and all metal parts are chromium-plated.

.... The cost of the new Hospital, including all new roads, all fees, laying out of grounds, etc., is approximately £21,500, and the cost of furnishing and equipment is £2,800, making a total finished cost per bed of just over £600.

W. D. C.

When MacDiarmid was hospitalised, four years later, Dr Chambers remained the Physician-Superintendent. His Deputy at this time was Dr James Valentine, who had joined the staff in 1933. MacDiarmid already knew Dr Valentine, as along with MacDiarmid he had been one of the founders of the National Party of Scotland. Dr Valentine left in November 1937. In his Report for the year ending 31st March, 1938, Dr Chambers wrote:

> *He was an excellent medical officer and a most agreeable colleague and his departure was deeply and sincerely regretted by everyone, though all congratulate him on his promotion and look forward with confidence to his further progress. In addition to sound judgment and admirable tact, he had a wide knowledge of clinical medicine as well as of psychiatry and psychology, and his clinical work, especially in the latter sphere,*

was of the first class. He was energetic and unsparing in support of the Hockey and Cricket Clubs, of both of which he was Captain and a most valuable playing member.

The Gilgal Hospital still stands on the grounds of Murray Royal Hospital. Although now in disuse and boarded up, its architecture still delights and together with its beautiful surroundings, stands as testament to an era of hospital building (antithetical to today's Private Finance Initiative hospital building programme), when environment, quality construction and craftsmanship were valued as contributions to patient care.

The Gilgal, today.

Appendix IV:
Letter penned by Christopher Murray Grieve

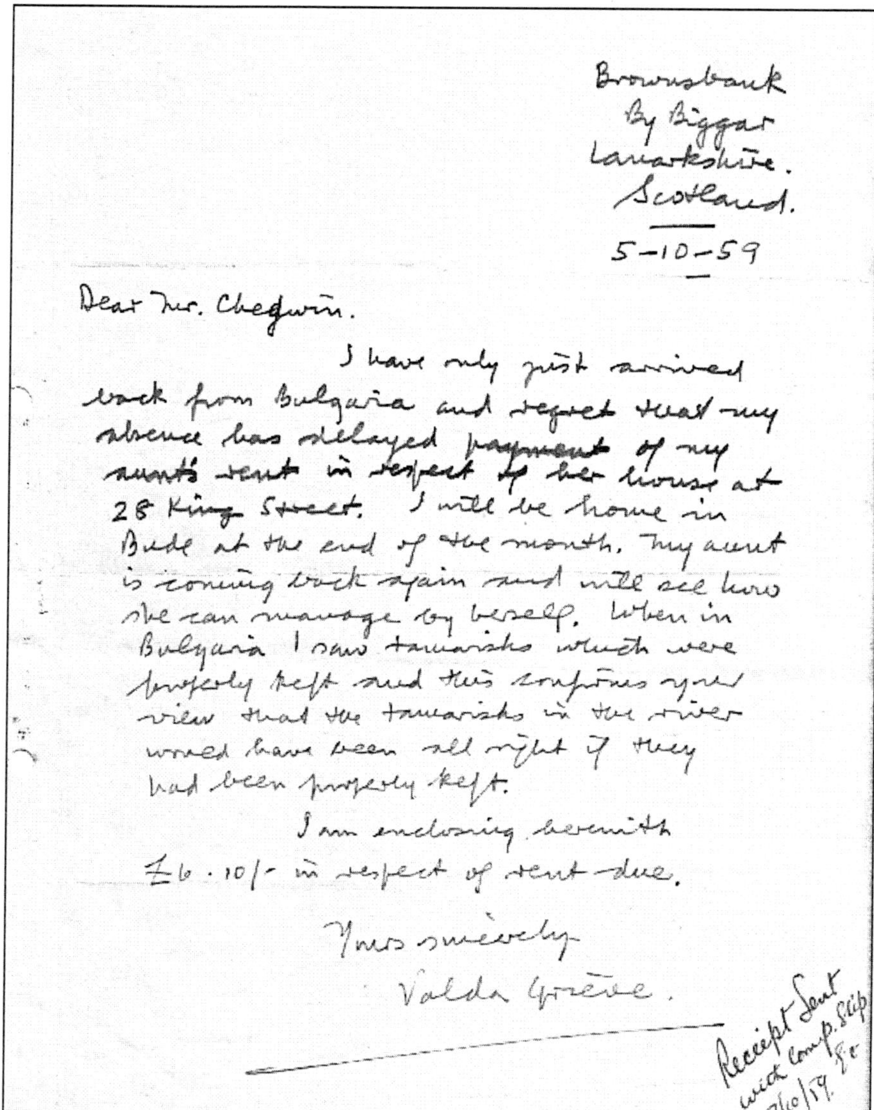

Brownsbank
By Biggar
Lanarkshire.
Scotland.

5-10-59

Dear Mr. Chegwin.

I have only just arrived back from Bulgaria and regret that my absence has delayed payment of my aunt's rent in respect of her house at 28 King Street. I will be home in Bude at the end of the month. My aunt is coming back again and will see how she can manage by herself. When in Bulgaria I saw tamarisks which were properly kept and this confirms your view that the tamarisks in the river would have been all right if they had been properly kept.

I am enclosing herewith £6.10/- in respect of rent due.

Yours sincerely

Valda Grieve.

Receipt Sent with Comp. Slip 7/10/59. E.C.

List of MacDiarmid's Works Referred to

List of MacDiarmid's Work Referred to

List of Works Consulted by the Editor

List of Works Consulted by the Editor

The Blanchminster Trust: A Cornish Charity, by Kathleen Beswetherick (Bude, Cornwall: The Blanchminster Trust, 1991).

Hugh MacDiarmid (C.M. Grieve), by Kenneth Buthlay, Scottish Writers Series, editor David Daiches (Edinburgh: Scottish Academic Press, 1982).

Daily Express, Thursday May 24 1934.

Daily Mail, May 1933.

The Decachord: A Magazine for Poetry-Lovers, edited by Charles John Arnell / Philippa Hole (1924-46).

England Census Record, 1891.

England Census Record, 1901.

A Meeting of Two Minds: Geddes Tagore Letters, edited and introduced by Bashabi Fraser (Edinburgh: Word Power Books, 2005).

Where Have All the Intellectuals Gone? Confronting 21st Century Philistinism, by Frank Furedi (London: Continuum, 2004).

The Glasgow Herald, 25 May 1989, p. 2.

Poems Addressed to Hugh MacDiarmid and Presented to him on his Seventy-fifth Birthday, preface by Sir Compton MacKenzie, edited with an introduction by Duncan Glen, drawings by Leonard Penrice (Preston: Akros Publications, 11 August 1967).

MacDiarmid in Shetland, edited by Laurence Graham and Brian Smith (Lerwick: Shetland Library, 1992).

Valda Grieve papers in the National Library of Scotland:

MS 27149; MS 27150; MS 27221 – 39;

Acc. 11857; Acc. 10488/1; Acc. 10533;

Acc. 10374/1 (Alan Bold's correspondence);

Acc. 12310/1 (Sam Gilliland correspondence);

MS 295 3 (amongst papers of Sorley MacLean).

Edinburgh University Library:

MS 2961.11 f. 8.

Collected Poems, Norman MacCaig, (London: Chatto & Windus. The Hogarth Press, 1985).

Scots as a Literary Medium: Point of View for Burns Day by C.M. Grieve (Hugh MacDiarmid), and subsequent articles & correspondence from *The Bulletin*, January 1938, reprinted in *Scottish Studies Review*, 6/1, Spring 2005, pp. 59-73.

Lucky Poet: A Self-Study in Literature and Political Ideas BEING THE AUTOBIOGRAPHY OF HUGH MACDIARMID (Christopher Murray Grieve), Hugh MacDiarmid (London: Methuen & Co. Ltd., 1943).

Hugh MacDiarmid Reads His Own Poetry, Claddagh Records Ltd., 1968.

The Letters of Hugh MacDiarmid, edited with an introduction by Alan Bold (London: Hamilton, 1984).

Hugh MacDiarmid: Selected Poetry, edited by Alan Riach and Michael Grieve (Manchester: Carcanet Press Ltd., 1992).

Complete Poems (2 Volumes), Hugh MacDiarmid, edited by Michael Grieve and W.R. Aitken (Manchester: Carcanet Press Ltd., 1994).

New Selected Letters, edited by Dorian Grieve, Owen Dudley Edwards and Alan Riach (Manchester: Carcanet Press, 2001).

The Revolutionary Art of the Future: Rediscovered Poems by *Hugh MacDiarmid,* edited by John Manson, Dorian Grieve and Alan Riach (Manchester: Carcanet Press in association with the Scottish Poetry Library, 2003).

MacDiarmid's Disciple, by Henry Mair (Kilwinning: Westward Media Ltd., 2001).

After Sixty Years: Once More on the Grieves in Whalsay, 1933-42 by John Manson, in *The New Shetlander Voar* Issue 2003 (No. 233).

Hugh MacDiarmid in England (1929-34) by John Manson, in *Markings* Issue 20/21, 2005.

Unquiet World: The Life of Count Geoffrey Potocki de Montalk, by Stephanie de Montalk (Victoria University of Wellington: Victoria University Press, 2001).

Murray's Asylum Reports 1927-1935 (Perth: J. Young & Sons).

Hugh MacDiarmid: The Tribute of the National Library of Scotland (pamphlet accompanying exhibition in 1967 to celebrate MacDiarmid's 75th birthday) (Edinburgh: National Library of Scotland, 1967).

Justice as Fairness / A Restatement, John Rawls, edited by Erin Kelly (London & Cambridge, Massachusetts: The Belknap Press of Harvard University Press, 2001).

Valda: The Struggles and Spirit of a Fighting Celt by Raymond Ross in *The Scotsman* (Sat. 1 September, 1984, p. 6).

Crying Out to be Written by Alan Riach, in *Folio* (National Library of Scotland, Issue 4, Spring 2002).

The Body's Rapture, by Jules Romains, translated from the French (*Psyché*) by John Rodker (New York: Liveright Publishing Corporation, 1933), (Black & Gold Edition, September 1937).

Jean-Paul Sartre: Basic Writings, edited by Stephen Priest (London: Routledge, 2001).

The Scotsman, 25 May 1989, p. 2 & p. 3.

Songs of Francis George Scott, 1880 – 1958: A Centenary Album of Forty-one Songs for Solo Voice and Piano selected and edited by Neil Mackay (Roberton Publications, 1980).

The Strange Life of August Strindberg, by Elizabeth Sprigge (London: Hamish Hamilton, 1949).

Married: Twenty Stories of Married Life, August Strindberg, authorised translation by Ellie Schleussner (London: Frank Palmer, 1913).

Brownsbank Cottage is now a museum owned by the Biggar Museum Trust and home to a writer-in-residence. It is open all year, but visits are by prior appointment only. Tel: 01899 221050; web site www.brownsbank.org.uk; Brownsbank Cottage, Candymill, Biggar, South Lanarkshire, ML12 6DT

The cottage the Grieves lived in on Whalsay is now a Camping Böd run by the Shetland Amenity Trust.

Index

Index

A page number followed by the letter 'n' indicates footnote reference.

H

I

J

K

T

U

V

W

Y